Arthurian Poets

MATTHEW ARNOLD AND WILLIAM MORRIS

THE GREAT REVIVAL of interest in the nineteenth century in the legends of King Arthur owes much to the poetry of Matthew Arnold and William Morris, whose major Arthurian work is included in this book.

Arnold's *Tristram and Iseult*, published in 1852, is the first modern English retelling of the legend, a melancholy interpretation of the theme. In particular, Arnold brings the character of Iseult of the White Hands to life, and his introduction of the two children sounds a pervasively poignant note; the resolution to the story reveals something of Arnold's pessimism about his age.

Morris takes up the second Arthurian triangle in *The Defence of Guenevere*; in this and his other poems – *King Arthur's Tomb, Sir Galahad: A Christmas Mystery*, and *The Chapel in Lyoness* – Morris examines the Arthurian stories from a psychological perspective and explores the emotional force behind the traditional responses. In their rich sensuality the poems demonstrate why the middle ages became so alluring to the pre-Raphaelites and their successors.

JAMES CARLEY is Professor of Medieval Studies, York University, Toronto.

Arthurian Poets

ALGERNON CHARLES SWINBURNE
Introduced by James P. Carley

EDWIN ARLINGTON ROBINSON
Introduced by James P. Carley

Arthurian Poets

MATTHEW ARNOLD

AND

WILLIAM MORRIS

Introduced by
JAMES P. CARLEY

THE BOYDELL PRESS

First published 1990 by The Boydell Press, Woodbridge
Reprinted 1995

Transferred to digital printing

ISBN 978-0-85115-544-9

The Boydell Press is an imprint of Boydell & Brewer Ltd
PO Box 9, Woodbridge, Suffolk IP12 3DF, UK
and of Boydell & Brewer Inc.
668 Mt Hope Avenue, Rochester, NY 14620, USA
website: www.boydellandbrewer.com

A CiP catalogue record for this book is available
from the British Library

This publication is printed on acid-free paper

CONTENTS

INTRODUCTION

The nineteenth century saw a great revival of interest in the Middle Ages, especially in all matters Arthurian. At the beginning of the century Malory's *Morte Darthur* was virtually unknown and more or less unattainable – the last edition had been published in 1634. Between 1816 and 1900, however, there were at least ten different editions of the Caxton text of Malory. For the pre-Raphaelites, in particular, the *Morte Darthur* became a kind of Bible and Georgiana Burne-Jones reported about her husband and his friend William Morris that 'sometimes I think that the book never can have been loved as it was by those two men. With Edward it became literally part of himself.' Later the Burne-Jones copy of Robert Southey's 1817 edition circulated widely among all the members of the pre-Raphaelite group and their friends: it was probably used by Ford Maddox Brown, by Dante Gabriel Rossetti and by Algernon Charles Swinburne, who wrote to Burne-Jones: 'Many thousand thanks for the precious loan – I hardly liked to ask for that little copy, knowing its nearness and dearness to you'.

Given the passion for Malory, then, it is suprising to discover that Matthew Arnold (1822–1888) did not base his 'Tristram and Iseult' (published in *Empedocles on Etna, and Other Poems*, 1852, and the first modern English retelling of the Tristram legend) on this source. Rather, as his letter to Herbert Hill – dated 5 November, 1852 – makes clear, he turned to French materials:

I read the story of Tristram and Iseult some years ago at Thun in an article in a French review on the romance literature; I had never met with it before, and it fastened upon me; when I got back to England I looked at the 'Morte d'Arthur' and took what I could, but the poem was already in the main formed, and I could not well disturb it.

His primary source was Théodore de la Villemarque's 'Les poèmes gallois et les romans de la Table-Ronde' in the *Revue de Paris*, 3rd ser. xxiv (1841), 266–82, although for the Merlin/Vivian section he used La Villemarque's earlier article (1837): 'Visite au Tombeau de Merlin'. It was not until 1853 that he consulted John Colin Dunlop's *The History of Fiction* (3 vols; London, 1814), excerpts of which formed a preface to the edition of 1853.

Evocations of December, moonlight, and pallor permeate Arnold's 'Tristram and Iseult'; in the background, moreover, there is the image of the knight 'Alone and palely loitering' of Keats' 'La Belle Dame sans Merci' – a poem which William Morris claimed was 'the germ from which all the poetry of [their] group had sprung.' At the very beginning the narrator, a Breton bard, gives an unmistakable echoing: 'What Knight is this so weak and pale'. Later, Tristram 'is weak with fever and pain'; his companions at war call him 'moonstruck'; and, as we are reminded, 'There's a secret in his breast / Which will never let him rest.' Like Keats' Knight, Tristram is drawn to the wood for 'sick pining'. What the poem makes sadly apparent is that all the good will in the world cannot break spells. Tristram is courteous and caring, but his wife and children cannot reach him. After he cries out desperately and uncontrollably in fever for Iseult the Fair, he repentantly addresses Iseult of the White Hands as 'Sweet', as 'Poor Child'. He remembers his children but even they cannot permeate his *idée fixe*. The fantasy draws him on and their world must be left behind.

Fantasy, moreover, is a key word. Like Keats' 'The Eve of St Agnes' – of which there are many specific echoes – this is a tale of long ago. It is told retrospectively by the Breton bard, who reminds us that it is all 'Cold, cold as those who lived and loved/ A thousand years ago'. Within the framework of the main story itself there is also the 'old-world Breton history' told by Iseult of the White Hands. In her ability to transform unwelcome facts, Iseult of the White Hands is like Malory's Elaine – also tending her fevered knight – and even more like Tennyson's Lady of Shalott: 'Spinning with her maidens here, / Listlessly through the window-bars / Gazing seawards many a league, / From her lonely shore-built tower'. Unlike the case of the Lady, however, the spell is never broken. She retreats back to the Breton tales and the revenge on 'real' life which they offer.

In the opposition of the two Iseults there is a hint of the classic Victorian concern about the Eve/Mary contrast: one thinks in particular of Sir Joseph Noel Paton's *The Choice*, described by *The Art Journal* in 1895: 'A Knight completely armed in mail stands upon the verge of a precipice, grasping with his right hand the hand of an angel, while with his left he rejects the advances of a Circean temptress – a luridly beautiful, bold and attractive woman, arranged in luxurious deshabille'. One Iseult – proud, dark-eyed, raven-haired, petulant and quick in reply, Tristram's 'haughty Queen' – brings death, but the other – 'her looks . . . mild', a 'snowdrop by the sea', 'The sweetest Christian soul alive', 'lovely orphan child' – is stultifying, death-in-life.

When he wrote 'Tristram and Iseult', Arnold – as he later told Swinburne – did not know about the episode of the white and black sails, which forms a bitterly ironic climax in the traditional version. Tristram, languishing from a wound received from a poisoned lance, sends for Iseult the Fair to cure him. Overheard by Iseult of the White Hands, he asks the captain of the ship to raise white sails if Iseult is accompanying him on the return journey, black if she is not. When at last the ship is seen on the horizon Iseult of the White Hands, stung to fury by her husband's neglect, untruthfully reports that the sails are black. Heartbroken, Tristram dies; Iseult the Fair, arriving too late, also expires. Afterwards, the lovers are buried side by side and from the grave of Tristram grows a vine, from the grave of Iseult a rose.

In the medieval story, then, Iseult of the White Hands is finally driven to passionate action, which in turn leads to immediate revenge. Her passive role is expiated in one deed of white fury and, as an audience, we feel that she can now disappear from the scene, the tragedy completed. (Even in La Villemarque's synopsis Iseult tells Tristram that Iseult the Fair has refused to come to him.) Arnold's addition of part iii (about which he wrote: 'The story of Merlin, of which I am particularly fond, was brought in on purpose to relieve the poem, which would else I thought have ended too sadly') is extremely significant in this context. In Arnold's poem, where there is no violent repudiation of her former behaviour, Iseult of the White Hands remains incomplete, a kind of emotional loose-end after the lovers have died. The tale she tells a year later of Merlin and Vivian becomes an equivalent to her more dramatic action in other versions. In her recreation of the past she casts herself as the Vivian figure, Merlin the encaptured Tristram. At first one might be tempted to link Vivian, the scarlet magician – her mocking glee, flushed cheek and loosened hair – to Iseult the Fair rather than to her patient pale counterpart. In fact, however, the second Iseult refers specifically to Vivian's 'white right hand' (which parallels her own chief defining characteristic) and – in a broader framework – like Vivian with Merlin, her persistence ultimately yielded her the prize she was seeking. What she got, of course, became a shadow of the old Tristram – his harp, his forest dress, his bow laid aside – and one wonders if she did not become 'passing weary' of the kind of love he could give her, ultimately 'dying' inwardly herself in her external 'mask of youth'.

Weary, moreover, is an operative word here: part iii, in particular, is a sustained invocation of melancholy exhaustion, lack of colour and action. The children, once again Arnold's addition, add to the mood of poignant sadness: 'helpless birds in the warm nest', 'two angel-heads', 'tired madcaps' and so forth. Their sweet little heads, their expectant dreams, their innocent play in the woods stand in sharp contrast to their inability to touch their father effectively and their inability to bring their mother back to any kind of vibrant life after his death.

Without the black sails episode it is possible for Arnold to introduce a last meeting between Tristram and Iseult the Fair and part ii of the poem is devoted to a sad dialogue, a tale 'of true, long-parted lovers,/ Join'd at evening of their days again.' Here, the lovers compare their lots and conclude that both were equally miserable: 'Thee, a pining exile in thy forest/ Me, a smiling queen upon my throne'. In part i, Arnold used Tristram's fevered hallucinations as a flashback technique to outline Tristram's adventures after his departure from Iseult – and one must remember that the Tristram story was relatively unknown to Arnold's audience. In part ii, the narrator sketches in 'proud' Iseult's life at Tintagel and King Mark's court. We have her feverish excitement – 'With hot-flush'd cheeks and brilliant eyes' – succeeded by melancholy – 'As pale and still as wither'd flowers'. Like Tristram himself, she seems consumed by a kind of hectic passion which makes the rest of the court draw away, seek Christ's protection 'from such fantasy'.

The fantasy theme ties in with the philosophical burden in part iii. The lovers are quite obviously burned out; their single-minded passion makes 'All which we did before, shadow and dream.' This, our commentator tells us, is waste: 'it angers me to see / How this fool passion gulls men potently; / Being, in truth, but a diseased unrest, / And an unnatural overheat at best.' As the tale makes clear, action is denied them, but they are not alone in this dilemma; we in the 'modern world' face a similar situation: 'the furnace of the world' has made us crumbled and has left 'the fierce necessity to feel, / But takes away the power – this can avail, / By drying up our joy in everything.' The solution, so the poem suggests but never fully articulates, seems to lie in the 'palace of art' and it is perhaps no coincidence that each section ends with a coda about the recreation of the past, tragic though it may be, through dreams, through tapestry, through story telling. In this sense the poem is a reaction against the 'unpoetrylessness' of Arnold's age and is a positive statement – even if it begins and ends with melancholy poignancy: Tristram's 'not the Iseult I desire' and Vivian 'passing weary of his love'.

Nor should the whole question of the transforming power of art be taken as a mere literary device. Like Morris in his choice of the Arthur/Lancelot/Guenevere story, Arnold discovered in the Tristram/Iseult the Fair/Iseult of the White Hands a myth which reflected his own experience and which could be used, molded and reinterpreted, as an artistic commentary on his own life. The parallels between Tristram and his Iseults and Arnold's own situation at the time of composition have been often pointed out. In September 1848, Arnold appears to have followed a certain Mary Clare – 'Marguerite' as he calls her – to Thun in Switzerland. In 1849 he once again returned to Thun and his beloved 'Marguerite', about whom he composed a series of poems. By 1850, however, he was courting Frances Lucy Wightman, who would soon become his wife, and 'Absence' signals the end of the Marguerite poems. What seem uncanny in the context of the Tristram story are the names themselves. On one hand, we have the beautiful Marguerite – the shining white pearl, the enchanting daisy whose blood came 'flushing to thy languid cheek'; on the other we have Wightman – of the white hands (i.e. 'mains') – and the implicit pun seems almost shocking in its appropriateness. As in so many of the nineteenth-century retellings of the Arthurian tales, life seems determined to imitate art, even down to specific details.

William Morris (1834–1896) first discovered the *Morte Darthur* in 1855 and was immediately and powerfully drawn to Malory's Arthurian world. He planned to write a complete Arthuriad but this never came to fruition and the four initial poems in *The Defence of Guenevere and Other Poems* (1858) –

'The Defence of Guenevere', 'King Arthur's Tomb', 'Sir Galahad, A Christmas Mystery', 'The Chapel in Lyoness' – remain his major poetic statement on the subject. There are, nevertheless, other Arthurian sections in this – Morris' first – anthology: the short evocative 'Near Avalon', the rescue of Sir Guy by Lancelot in 'A Good Knight in Prison', and the ballad about Lancelot in 'Sir Peter Harpdon's End'. Various fragments – such as 'The Maying of Guenevere', planned as the first poem of the putative Arthurian cycle – also survive.

To recreate an old romance, so Morris argued, the writer should 'Read it through . . . then shut the book and write it out again as a new story for yourself'. 'The Defence of Guenevere' shows a particularly successful application of this technique. The actual scene which Morris is dramatizing occurs towards the end of Malory's work:

> and thenne the quene was led forth withoute Carleil. And there she was despoylled into her smok, and soo thenne her ghoostly fader was broughte to her to be shryuen of her mysdedes. Thenne was there wepynge and waylynge and wryngynge of handes of many lordes and ladyes, but there were but fewe in comparyson that wold bere ony armour for to strengthe the dethe of the quene.
>
> Thenne was ther one that Sire Launcelot had sente vnto that place for to aspye what tyme the quene shold goo vnto her dethe, and anone as he sawe the quene despoylled into her smok, and so shryuen, thenne he gaf Sir Launcelot warnynge. Thenne was there but sporynge and pluckynge vp of horses, and ryghte so they cam to the fyre . . .

Malory's prose is terse and action-laden: this scene leads directly to the next event, Lancelot's rescue of Guenevere and its more important consequence, the inevitable breakup of the Round Table. In Malory's world of adventure, Guenevere's feelings are unexplored: indeed, Arthur himself will later make it quite clear that she is at best a pawn, certainly unimportant in the greater world of his fellowship: 'for quenes I myghte haue ynowe, but suche a felaushyp of good knyghtes shalle neuer be togyders in no company.'

Apart from this main episode there are other references to Malory – to Gawaine's mother Morgause, for example, killed by Gaheris in the *Morte Darthur* rather than by Aggravayne as 'The Defence' relates. (This change was probably a lapse of memory on Morris' part rather than a deliberate deviation from his source.) More specifically, Guenevere herself recalls Lancelot's duel with Mellyagraunce, Guenevere's abductor, an episode which derives ultimately from Chrétien de Troyes' *Knight of the Cart*. In Malory, even more than in Chretien, the focus is on Lancelot as hero. In Morris' version, on the other hand, we see everything from Guenevere's perspective; the poem dramatises her reactions, violent and sensuous, to the events. The summer heat is emphasized, as is her fascination with fire and blood. Unlike Malory, where Gawaine is unmentioned in this scene, Guenevere asserts that he was present and bitterly reminds him that he, like all the others, 'held his [Mellyagraunce's] word without a flaw'.

In Malory's 'Slander and Strife' it is Mordred and Aggravayne who storm Guenevere's room after they have persuaded Arthur to set a trap for the lovers. Gawaine has no part in the plot and is, in fact, strongly loyal to Lancelot and Guenevere. He argues passionately in defence of the queen:

> my lord Arthur, I wold counceylle yow not to be ouer hasty, but that ye wold putte it in respyte, this iugement of my lady the quene, for many causes. One it is, though it were so that Sir Launcelot were fonde in the quenes chamber, yet it myghte be soo that he came thyder for none euylle. For ye knowe, my lord, said Syr Gawayne, that the quene is moche beholden vnto Syr Launcelot more than vnto ony other knyghte, for oftymes he hath saued her lyf and done batail for her whan al the courte refused the quene. And parauenture she sente for hym for goodenes and for none euyl, to rewarde hym for his good dedes that he had done to her in tymes past. And peraduenture my lady the quene sente for hym to that entente, that Syr Launcelot shold come to her good grace pryuely and secretely, wenynge

to her that hit was best so to do in eschewyng and dredyng of sklaunder. For oftymes we doo many thynges that we wene it be for the best, and yet peraduenture hit torneth to the werst. For I dare say, sayd Syre Gawayne, my lady your quene is to yow bothe good and true. And as for Sir Launcelot, sayd Sir Gawayne, I dare saye he wylle make hit good vpon ony knyghte lyuyng that wylle putte vpon hymself vylony or shame, and in lyke wyse he wylle make good for my lady Dame Gueneuer.

When the judgement against Guenevere is irrevocably made Gawaine retreats tearfully to his chamber in an act of passive resistance. It is not until Lancelot's rescue of Guenevere, when Lancelot accidentally kills Gawaine's brothers Gaherys and Gareth, that Gawaine turns against his old mentor and hero. Gawaine as chief prosecutor, then, is entirely a creation of Morris. Why this change? Here, perhaps, it is a question of Morris responding to the general tone of Malory's denouement in spite of, or even in opposition to, specific facts of the narrative sequence. At the end of the *Morte Darthur* – after Guenevere's rescue – Gawaine does indeed become an unforgiving and violent individual, the character who in some ways because of his refusal to permit any kind of reconciliation must be held responsible for the actual violent collapse of the Round Table. It is this stubbornly embittered Gawaine, incapable of forgiveness, who becomes an appropriate accusor of Guenevere. The facts are wrong, in other words, and the matière transformed, but the 'psychological' sens is the same.

In actual form, 'The Defence of Guenevere' is a dramatic monologue. From the sudden beginning, *in medias res*, Guenevere is vividly present, every gesture richly highlighted. Both the poet and the character herself force us to look at her alone – except on the few occasions she directs us, usually contemptuously, to particular members of her audience. Legalistic although many of the arguments are – and note Guenevere's brilliant use of 'still', 'but', 'nevertheless' – there is also a great emotional power and erotic intensity. At the very beginning of the poem Guenevere's cheek which 'burned so' makes us think of the slap of a glove to mark a challenge to a duel. There is another level, however; at this point it is well within the bounds of possibility that her cheek will be literally burning before long. The fire of the stake is always in the background and it is this, along with a kind of underlying liebestod motif, which accounts for the quality of delirium to which Walter Pater, for example, so perceptively refers.

The defence itself takes several forms. Guenevere's main point, strictly legalistic, is that Gawaine is incorrect in this particular accusation (but note the movement from 'Whatever may have happened through these years' to 'Whatever happened on through all those years'): she and Lancelot were not indulging in a coital embrace when the knights burst into her chamber. (In this kind of tricking prevarication one is reminded of Lancelot's earlier challenge of Mellyagraunce's point that the blood in Guenevere's bed came from one of the knights sleeping in her room. There is also the beggar episode in the Tristan and Isolde story.) Guenevere, a seasoned rhetorician, begins with an emotional appeal to establish herself as victim rather than villain. She presents the image of the choosing cloths and her innocent miscalculation. She then moves to Arthur's great name and little love, and also reminds us that human love is the stairway to heaven. If she didn't have Lancelot, she would be in a kind of spiritual limbo and incapable ever of ascending to God. The tone now established, we move from metaphor and metaphysical speculation to a specific episode in her past, full of erotic detail – the heat of the enclosed garden, the beauty of her hand, the mouths which 'went wandering in one way' and so forth. Just as we appear to be approaching the ultimate revelation, however, we break off at line 142 – in a pattern which will be repeated – with the sharp refrain 'Nevertheless you, O Sir Gauwaine, lie'.

In a technique not dissimilar to Chaucer's Pardoner in her manipulation of her audience through calculated degrees of self-revelation, Guenevere now points out that 'A great queen

such as I / Having sinn'd this way, straight her conscience
sears; / And afterwards she liveth hatefully, / Slaying and
poisoning'. (This, of course, brings to mind the episodes with
which she is associated in various sections of Malory.)
Gawaine, fully bewitched so she hopes, is directly invited to
'speak me lovingly' and pity her. When he turns away in disgust, we move back to narrative and have the Mellyagrance
story and the sharp reminder to the knights that it is dangerous
to accuse one so beautiful. This leads to yet another paean to
her own beauty, terminated when it is clear that the knightly
accusors are not falling under the spell. And so at last we come
to the episode of her arrest, which is recounted in intimate
detail. But, suddenly, just as she is about to repeat the speech
made by Lancelot (as interesting and provocatively new to us
as the poem's external audience as to the knights within the
poem), she stops – like Iago she will not speak another word –
and, more to the point, she has heard Lancelot coming. The
story is over; a defence is no longer needed. In fact, the whole
narrative has been a playing for time, a variation on the
Scheherazade theme. In the end Guenevere, the consummate
actress – carefully modulating her voice and watching every
reaction of her audience – knows it is all just a story: the
crimson of her cheek caused by the challenge in the opening is
exchanged for the excitement and flush on her cheek as Lancelot appears.

The colour imagery is extremely important, as one might
expect in the poetry of a man who said about thirteenth-century
illuminated manuscripts: 'Nothing can exceed . . . the loveliness of the colour found at this period in the best-executed
books.' We have the heraldic cloths and her seemingly
innocent identification with blue as the colour of faithfulness in
contrast to the passion of red. Elsewhere, too, crimson in all its
ambiguities is emphasized: shame (as she touches her cheek),
fire (as she wonders how the flames would quiver above her
head as she burned at the stake), pride (as she lifts her head
with its burning cheek aloft), sexual excitement (as her cheek

grows crimson when she hears Lancelot). Crimson as fire also ties in with the blood imagery: her hand against the sun, her full blooded lips, blood on the sheets and all its sexual connotations, her breast rising 'Like waves of purple sea', the excitement of the kill (when Mellyagraunce was slain in the heat of summer). White, surprisingly, is linked ambiguously with red. It is most obviously the colour of purity: hands white 'as when you wed' in opposition to blood stained sheets. The whitened winter without Lancelot, however, is explicitly contrasted with summer when 'I grew white with flame'. Finally, we have the white fear of Mellyagraunce which curdled his blood and then led to the 'spout of blood on the hot land'.

'The Defence of Guenevere' is most obviously a 'modern' recreation of a section of the *Morte Darthur*. It describes a sensuous, highly sexual character, one almost solipsistic in her admiration of her own beauty and the havoc it wreaks; it is this aspect, perhaps, which prompted a contemporary reviewer in *The Athenaeum* to observe that the poem shows 'how far affectation may mislead an earnest man towards the fog-land of Art.' At another level, though, the poem is an attempt to show how the storyteller can enrapture an audience – and herself too at times – regardless of objective truth or moral purpose. Ultimately, 'The Defence of Guenevere' is, as Northrop Frye has observed elsewhere concerning *The Earthly Paradise*, about the 'understanding that the telling and retelling of the great stories, in the face of the accusing memory, is a central part of the only battle that there is any point in fighting.'

'King Arthur's Tomb' takes its origin in two emotionally charged scenes from 'The Dolorous Death and Departing' conclusion of the *Morte Darthur*. The kingdom destroyed and Arthur dead, Lancelot visits the tomb of Gawaine at the castle of Dover. He then vows to seek out Guenevere. After a lonely quest of 'a seven or eyght dayes' he at last finds her in a nunnery at Amesbury. In the presence of all her ladies Guenevere denounces their great love and commands Lancelot never to see her again. More surprisingly, and seemingly heartlessly, she also tells him 'goo to thy royame, and there take the a wyf and lyue with hir with ioye and blysse.' Stunned and insulted by this suggestion, Lancelot swears that he too will forsake the world; he does, however, ask one last boon: 'Wherfore, madame, I praye you kysse me, and neuer no more.' This she refuses to do and they separate forever, swooning and weeping. True to his vow Lancelot devotes himself to a life of penance and fasting until the death of Guenevere, when he takes her to be buried with Arthur at Glastonbury. His spirit now fully broken, he awaits his own death: 'Euer he was lyeng grouelyng on the tombe of Kyng Arthur and Quene Gueneuer, and there was no comforte that the bysshop nor Syr Bors nor none of his felowes coude make hym; it auaylled not.'

This latter episode inspired Dante Gabriel Rossetti's water-colour, *Arthur's Tomb* (a painting which Morris bought from Rossetti) and this, in turn, was the immediate catalyst for Morris' poem. Once again, the changes and adaptations are revealing. In particular, combining the two scenes and shifting the meeting of Guenevere and Lancelot to Glastonbury and Arthur's tomb itself adds drama to the poem and leads to a heightening of atmosphere, at times a sense of cosmic irony almost as bitter as that found in Thomas Hardy's novels.

In Malory Guenevere appears concerned with her own sal-vation at the expense of Lancelot's feelings and loyalties. Malory, however, does not probe the possible turmoil behind her public queenly role. Morris' Guenevere, on the other hand, is completely divided between her public stance and her private sentiments. Part of the tension of 'King Arthur's Tomb' comes from the play between her articulated statements and her intimate reflection upon them. Sometimes it is difficult to dis-tinguish just who is speaking; certainly it is not always obvious whether Guenevere is addressing Lancelot or making an aside. Readers as sympathetic as Swinburne have taken this as a failing – and Swinburne, in particular, complained that the poem lacks 'joists and screws, props and rafters'. In fact, what it actually does, I think, is to increase the reader's disorientation in a manner similar to the rising frenzy in the characters themselves.

In Malory it is mentioned that both Guenevere and Lancelot 'swoun' at their parting and that Lancelot is still unconscious when Guenevere's ladies 'bare the quene to hir chambre.' In 'King Arthur's Tomb' the distraught Guenevere fears that she has literally killed Lancelot at this point in her determined repudiation and taunting – 'Now I have slain him, Lord, let me go too, I pray' – and she runs off in panic. The 'let me go too' is key: assuming that Lancelot is dead, she wants to share his fate. In the 'bell' which Lancelot hears upon awakening, there is perhaps a hint that her last prayer has been answered: in my reading, at least, this may well be the bell tolling the news of her own death. The 'bell / Of her mouth on my cheek' which once caused Lancelot to be overwhelmed and transfixed as when Enoch was translated to heaven has been exchanged for her death bell. (As Elisabeth Brewer points out, however, the bell might alternatively come from Malory: 'And Syr Launcelot awok, and went and took his hors, and rode al that day and al nyght in a forest wepyng. And atte last he was ware of an ermytage and a chappel stode betwyxte two clyffes, and than he herde a lytel belle rynge to Masse.')

Telling stories has very different effects in this poem from those in its companion piece. At the beginning Lancelot finds fiction an ineffectual insulation against the pain of his burning desire to get to Guenevere. He measures out tales to pass the long journey to Glastonbury, but in the end 'Still night, and night, and night, and emptied heart/ Of any stories; what a dismal load/ Time grew at last . . .' Guenevere, meanwhile, has determined to refuse his vision of their past, to destroy the remembered world that he is coming to confirm. Admitting freely to their adultery – 'This thing we did while yet he was alive' – she now uses words as weapons rather than as spells and we watch Lancelot twist as her haughty reproaches drive into him. 'Will she lie now, Lord God?' he cries out in horror. As in 'The Defence of Guenevere' Guenevere is acutely aware of audience – this time Lancelot and Our Lord himself – to each of whom she addresses different and conflicting discussions. (Pater is particularly interesting on this topic. 'The Arthurian legends', he states, 'pre-Christian in their origin, yield all their sweetness only in a Christian atmosphere. What is characteristic in them is the strange suggestion of a deliberate choice between Christ and a rival lover.') For her own salvation, as she sees it, Guenevere plays the prosecutor now, but is almost driven over the edge in doing so: 'I shall go mad,/ Or else die kissing him'. In 'The Defence of Guenevere' Guenevere reconstructed the past to enchant her audience and to beguile them: stories passed the time until her rescuer appeared. In 'King Arthur's Tomb' she destroys the past, unravels the web, in order to escape from the consequences of her great love. To obtain heaven – to have both Christ and Lancelot (not to mention Arthur) – the whole fabric of the past must be repudiated. When the 'life illusion', as John Cowper Powys calls it, is removed, is destroyed, however, the consequence is a blinding void – unconsciousness, perhaps death itself.

Grey, the colour of autumn, penance and death, predominates in 'King Arthur's Tomb': both Lancelot and Guenevere have to submit to the kind of oblivion it brings – 'no colours then'. When stories fail, Lancelot is confronted with 'the lone / Grey horse's head before him' and 'the grey road'. In the same morning twilight, moreover, 'the grey downs bare' transform themselves into 'lumps of sin' for Guenevere. The greenery of spring and summer, 'the old garden life' is gone. The scarlet robes to which Guenevere referred in 'The Defence of Guenevere' have been replaced by a nun's black robes and white veil. Dusty and tired Lancelot too remembers his own former 'red robe' – a reference which casts an ironic light on Guenevere's earlier explication of the choosing cloths scene and her identification of Lancelot with blue, Arthur with red. In 'The Defence of Guenevere' Guenevere's eyes were not a dull grey, but the alluring grey of the typical heroine of medieval romance; the greyness of weeping tightly associated with 'me, being so beautiful'. As grey has transformed itself in 'King Arthur's Tomb', though, so has red: it is now the colour of penance and Guenevere identifies herself with the Magdalene: 'Her dimmed eyes scorch'd and red . . . no gold light on her hair'.

'The Defence of Guenevere' and 'King Arthur's Tomb' are, then, a balanced pair, whose imagery is mutually reflecting, and they fit closely together. If 'The Defence of Guenevere' is about the success of storytelling 'King Arthur's Tomb' is about its ultimate failure. If 'The Defence of Guenevere' is about the heat of summer 'King Arthur's Tomb' is about the onset of autumn. If 'The Defence of Guenevere' is about the integration of red and white, 'scarlet lilies', then 'King Arthur's Tomb' shows the ultimate triumph of grey, indeed the repudiation of colour altogether. As David Riede has pointed out: 'The two poems that introduce the volume, then, introduce its insistent theme: though we must long for the simplicity and beauty of 'old romance,' we are constantly returned to a world of 'wormy circumstance,' and more, that the most we gain from attempting to escape into a world of romance is a longer imprisonment, a metaphoric stay of execution.'

As the first pair of poems in *The Defence of Guenevere and Other Poems* take the adulterous Guenevere and her emblem of scarlet lilies as their focus, so too do the second pair examine her opposite, the chaste Sir Galahad, the Red Cross Knight. White on red, as it were, is exchanged for red on white. From his first appearance in the *Lancelot-Grail* prose cycle the figure of Gahalad has created major literary problems. How does one render believable or even mildly engaging a character whose actions and whose very name ('Galeed' = 'cairn of witness') proclaim him at every step to be an allegory for purity? Morris' response to Tennyson's Galahad – 'rather a mild youth' – applies equally to the hero of the medieval French *Queste del Saint Graal*, to Malory's Galahad, and to the anemic hero of so many nineteenth century pictorial renditions. Nevertheless, Morris himself had originally been attracted by the monastic

ideal which he saw Galahad embodying. 'Remember', wrote
his friend Burne Jones to Cormell Price, 'I have set my heart on
our founding a brotherhood. Learn Sir Galahad by heart. He is
to be the patron of our order.'

Most obviously, 'Sir Galahad, A Christmas Mystery' shows
that the wooden character of the medieval romances had feelings under his inflexible exterior and – more importantly –
doubts, just as lesser individuals do. Galahad's internal dialogue leading up to the 'mystery' play of the Grail scene reveals Galahad's inner conflicts during his dark night of the
soul. That he came to the chapel 'Six hours ago' makes an
implicit equivalent with Christ's passion (leading up to His cry
from the Cross: 'My God, my God, why hast thou forsaken
me?') even more obvious; at the time of the Crucifixion 'from
the sixth hour there was darkness over all the land until the
ninth hour'.

In his loneliness Galahad wishes to be as other men. He
expresses this in terms of courtly love and sexuality.
Palyomydes has his love-sorrow for Iseult, Lancelot adores
Guenevere. Unlike these others, though, who can think about
their beloved's 'arms, round, / Warm and lithe', poor Galahad
– as he reminds himself in a bitter pun – will eventually be
found alone 'Dead in my arms'. What he laments, in fact, is the
power of fantasy. He wishes to have the right to dream in the
way normal individuals do, to be in a world of imagination
where any 'place / Grows very pleasant' through the thoughts
of the beloved. What Galahad's 'moodiness' does not let him
consider, however, is that fantasy works only temporarily: as
he will later be assured even Lancelot will eventually 'hang his
head'. It is Galahad's fate, then, to be able to see, not through a
glass darkly like normal individuals, but face to face: when the
Redeemer appears He tells Galahad to 'Rise up, and look and
listen . . . for you will see no frown / Upon my face', and He
reminds him 'no pride / Closes your eyes, no vain lust keeps
them down'.

The appearance of the angels and Galahad's dressing by the

holy ladies is based in part on Malory (where angels enter with
the Grail at King Pelles' castle and where Galahad goes to
Solomon's ship and sees the three spindles fixed to the head of
a mysterious bed containing a sword which had belonged to
King David) and in part on the traditional clothing ritual in-
volved in the initiation into knighthood. As Christ came to him
in the colour of both his major festivals – 'raiment half blood-
red, half white as snow' – so too do the angels arrive spotlessly
in white with scarlet wings, bearing a surcoat of white with a
red cross. The Grail vision, in fact, coalesces with an initiation
into pure spiritual knighthood. For Galahad, there is no need
for the period of blind human worldliness between Christmas
and Easter – birth to death. For him the vision can come all at
once.

In Malory the Grail quest signalled the beginning of the
collapse of the earthly fellowship of the Round Table. So too
does the rest of the world seem flat and empty after Galahad's
vision in 'Sir Galahad, A Christmas Mystery'. When his companions arrive – the three who, as in Malory, will accompany
him on his last journey – their news conveys the sense of the
waste land, of a world of 'bare twigs' where 'the many-
colour'd raiment' remains elusive. Dinadan, the storyteller is
dead, Lionel and Gauwaine are shamed, Lauvaine badly
wounded and all is in vain, no Grail experience possible for the
general companionship of the Round Table.

'The Chapel in Lyoness' was first published separately in
the September 1856 issue of the *Oxford and Cambridge
Magazine*. Many years later, just before the Ellis reprint of
1875, Morris made a number of alterations to the poem in his
own copy of *The Defence of Guenevere and Other Poems*, but
these were not in fact used in the Ellis edition. 'The Chapel in
Lyoness' is both the most inaccessible of the Arthurian group
in terms of narrative and the least directly linked to Malory.
What is important in this latter context, so it would seem, is not
any specific incident but the choice of Sir Ozana le Cure Hardy
as 'protagonist': in the medieval romances he is one of the most

obscure of the knights, often captured, unable to guard the
Queen or heal Sir Urre or find the missing Lancelot. He is, as
Curtis Dahl points out, 'second-rate', 'the ordinary unheroic
person.' His life and accomplishments as knight, in other
words, do need some sort of redemption, some sort of meaning
imposed.

The links between 'The Chapel in Lyoness' and 'Sir
Galahad, A Christmas Mystery' are pervasive: a movement
from Christmas-Eve to Whit-Sunday, the feast of the descent of
the Holy Spirit and the time of the original appearance of the
Grail at the court of King Arthur; the remote chapel in Lyoness;
and the samite cloth of white and red, reminding us of the
earlier half blood-red, half white 'raiment' in which Galahad
saw Christ attired.

'The Chapel in Lyoness' portrays Galahad in his role as
Christ substitute and the priestly kiss of peace leads to a final
confession, a hint of understanding for Ozana. (In the revised
version, moreover, Bors sees Galahad's shield outside the
chapel. This change emphasizes the parallels between the poem
and the various chapel episodes in the medieval accounts of
Galahad's Grail quest.) Through Galahad Ozana can move
from his earlier 'Ah! me, I cannot fathom it' to his dying 'Now
I begin to fathom it.' As Bors – the voice of the mixed life, the
only person able to see the Grail and return to the 'normal'
world – observes, moreover, when Ozana dies and is transfixed, then Galahad himself sees 'strange things' – a beatific
vision where Ozana is reunited with the mysterious fair (identi-
fied as his own sister whom he failed earlier by some commen-
tators, as the sister of Perceval by others) and where his hands
can twine within all 'the tresses of her hair', not just a single
detached 'golden tress'. Bors' cry for mercy as he observes
Galahad also reminds us, however, that those of vision are not
for this world – as in Coleridge's 'Kubla Khan' lesser individuals need to take warning:

Beware! Beware!
His flashing eyes, his floating hair!
Weave a circle round him thrice,
And close your eyes with holy dread,
For he on honeydew hath fed,
And drunk the milk of Paradise.

SELECT BIBLIOGRAPHY

MATTHEW ARNOLD

Brooks, Roger L. 'Matthew Arnold's Revision of *Tristram and Iseult*: Some Instances of Clough's Influence'. *Victorian Poetry* 2 (1964), 57–60.

Davis, Mary Byrd. 'A Source for Arnold's Tale of Merlin and Vivian'. *ELN* 14 (1976), 120–23.

Kendall, J. L. 'The Unity of Arnold's *Tristram and Iseult*'. *Victorian Poetry* 1 (1963), 140–45.

Leavy, Barbara Fass. 'Iseult of Britanny: A New Interpretation of Matthew Arnold's *Tristram and Iseult*'. *Victorian Poetry* 18 (1980), 1–22.

Riede, David G. *Matthew Arnold and the Betrayal of Language*. Charlottesville, Va., 1988.

Russ, Jon R. 'A Possible Source for the Death Scene in Arnold's *Tristram and Iseult*'. *Victorian Poetry* 9 (1971), 336–38.

Siegchrist, Mark. 'The Role of Vivian in Arnold's "Tristram and Iseult"'. *Criticism* 16 (1974), 136–52.

Sundell, M. G. 'The Intellectual Background and Structure of Arnold's *Tristram and Iseult*'. *Victorian Poetry* 1 (1963), 272–83.

Taylor, Beverly. 'Imagination and Art in Arnold's "Tristram and Iseult": The Importance of "Making"'. *Studies in English Literature 1500–1900* 22 (1982), 633–645.

WILLIAM MORRIS

Balch, Dennis R. 'Guenevere's Fidelity to Arthur in "The Defence of Guenevere" and "King Arthur's Tomb"'. *Victorian Poetry* 13 (1975), 61–70.

Berry, Ralph. 'A Defence of Guenevere'. *Victorian Poetry* 9 (1971), 277–86.

Calhoun, Blue. *The Pastoral Vision of William Morris: The Earthly Paradise*. Athens, Georgia, 1975.

Carson, Angela. 'Morris' Guenevere: A Further Note'. *Philological Quarterly* 42 (1963), 131–34.

Dahl, Curtis. 'Morris's "The Chapel in Lyoness"': An Interpretation'. *Studies in Philology* 51 (1954), 482–491.

Galyon, Aubrey E. 'William Morris: The Past as Standard'. *Philological Quarterly* 56 (1977), 245–49.

Perrine, Laurence. 'Morris's Guenevere: An Interpretation'. *Philological Quarterly* 39 (1960), 234–41.

Post, Jonathan F. S. 'Guenevere's Critical Performance'. *Victorian Poetry* 17 (1979), 317–27.

Raymond, Meredith B. 'The Arthurian Group in *The Defence of Guenevere and Other Poems*'. *Victorian Poetry* 4 (1966), 213–18.

Riede, David G. 'Morris, Modernism, and Romance'. *ELH* 51 (1984), 85–106.

Silver, Carole G. ' "The Defence of Guenevere"': A Further Interpretation'. *Studies in English Literature* 9 (1969), 695–702.

Spatt, Hartley S. 'William Morris and the Uses of the Past'. *Victorian Poetry* 13 (1975), 1–9.

Staines, David. 'Morris' Treatment of His Medieval Sources in *The Defence of Guenevere and Other Poems*'. *Studies in Philology* 70 (1973), 439–64.

Stallman, Robert L. 'The Lovers' Progress: An Investigation of William Morris' "The Defence of Guenevere" and "King Arthur's Tomb"'. *Studies in English Literature* 15 (1975), 657–70.

Tarvers, Josephine Koster. ' "The Deep Still Land of Colours"': Color Imagery in *The Defence of Guenevere and Other Poems*'. *Studies in Philology* 84 (1987), 180–193.

Tompkins, J. M. S. *William Morris: an Approach to the Poetry.* London, 1988 .

TRISTRAM AND ISEULT

TRISTRAM AND ISEULT [8]

I

𝔗ristram

Tristram

Is she not come? The messenger was sure.
Prop me upon the pillows once again—
Raise me, my page! this cannot long endure.
—Christ, what a night! how the sleet whips the pane!
What lights will those out to the northward be?

The Page

The lanterns of the fishing-boats at sea.

Tristram

Soft—who is that, stands by the dying fire?

Iseult.
　　　　　　　　The Page

　　　　　　　　Tristram

　　　Ah! not the Iseult I desire.

　　*　　　*　　　*　　　*

What Knight is this so weak and pale,
Though the locks are yet brown on his noble head,
Propt on pillows in his bed,
Gazing seaward for the light
Of some ship that fights the gale
On this wild December night?
Over the sick man's feet is spread
A dark green forest-dress;
A gold harp leans against the bed,
Ruddy in the fire's light.
I know him by his harp of gold,
Famous in Arthur's court of old;
I know him by his forest-dress—
The peerless hunter, harper, knight,
Tristram of Lyoness.

What Lady is this, whose silk attire
Gleams so rich in the light of the fire?
The ringlets on her shoulders lying
In their flitting lustre vying
With the clasp of burnish'd gold
Which her heavy robe doth hold.
Her looks are mild, her fingers slight
As the driven snow are white;
But her cheeks are sunk and pale.
Is it that the bleak sea-gale
Beating from the Atlantic sea
On this coast of Brittany,
Nips too keenly the sweet flower?
Is it that a deep fatigue
Hath come on her, a chilly fear,
Passing all her youthful hour
Spinning with her maidens here,

Listlessly through the window-bars
Gazing seawards many a league,
From her lonely shore-built tower,
While the knights are at the wars?
Or, perhaps, has her young heart
Felt already some deeper smart,
Of those that in secret the heart-strings rive,
Leaving her sunk and pale, though fair?
Who is this snowdrop by the sea?—
I know her by her mildness rare,
Her snow-white hands, her golden hair;
I know her by her rich silk dress,
And her fragile loveliness—
The sweetest Christian soul alive,
Iseult of Brittany.

Iseult of Brittany?—but where
Is that other Iseult fair,
That proud, first Iseult, Cornwall's queen?
She, whom Tristram's ship of yore
From Ireland to Cornwall bore,
To Tyntagel, to the side
Of King Marc, to be his bride?
She who, as they voyaged, quaff'd
With Tristram that spiced magic draught,
Which since then for ever rolls
Through their blood, and binds their souls,
Working love, but working teen?—
There were two Iseults who did sway
Each her hour of Tristram's day;
But one possess'd his waning time,
The other his resplendent prime.
Behold her here, the patient flower,

Who possess'd his darker hour!
Iseult of the Snow-White Hand
Watches pale by Tristram's bed.
She is here who had his gloom,
Where art thou who hadst his bloom?
One such kiss as those of yore
Might thy dying knight restore!
Does the love-draught work no more?
Art thou cold, or false, or dead,
Iseult of Ireland?

      *   *   *   *

Loud howls the wind, sharp patters the rain,
And the knight sinks back on his pillows again.
He is weak with fever and pain,
And his spirit is not clear.
Hark! he mutters in his sleep,
As he wanders far from here,
Changes place and time of year,
And his closéd eye doth sweep
O'er some fair unwintry sea,
Not this fierce Atlantic deep,
While he mutters brokenly :—

Tristram

The calm sea shines, loose hang the vessel's sails ;
Before us are the sweet green fields of Wales,
And overhead the cloudless sky of May.—
"*Ah, would I were in those green fields at play,*
Not pent on ship-board this delicious day!
Tristram, I pray thee, of thy courtesy,
Reach me my golden phial stands by thee,
But pledge me in it first for courtesy.—"

Ha! dost thou start? are thy lips blanch'd like mine?
Child, 'tis no true draught this, 'tis poison'd wine!
Iseult! . . . .

        *   *   *   *

    Ah, sweet angels, let him dream!
    Keep his eyelids! let him seem
    Not this fever-wasted wight
    Thinn'd and paled before his time,
    But the brilliant youthful knight
    In the glory of his prime,
    Sitting in the gilded barge,
    At thy side, thou lovely charge,
    Bending gaily o'er thy hand,
    Iseult of Ireland!
    And she too, that princess fair,
    If her bloom be now less rare,
    Let her have her youth again—
    Let her be as she was then!
    Let her have her proud dark eyes,
    And her petulant quick replies—
    Let her sweep her dazzling hand
    With its gesture of command,
    And shake back her raven hair
    With the old imperious air!
    As of old, so let her be,
    That first Iseult, princess bright,
    Chatting with her youthful knight
    As he steers her o'er the sea,
    Quitting at her father's will
    The green isle where she was bred,
    And her bower in Ireland,
    For the surge-beat Cornish strand;

Where the prince whom she must wed
Dwells on loud Tyntagel's hill,
High above the sounding sea.
And that potion rare her mother
Gave her, that her future lord,
Gave her, that King Marc and she,
Might drink it on their marriage-day,
And for ever love each other—
Let her, as she sits on board,
Ah, sweet saints, unwittingly!
See it shine, and take it up,
And to Tristram laughing say :
" Sir Tristram, of thy courtesy,
Pledge me in my golden cup!"
Let them drink it—let their hands
Tremble, and their cheeks be flame,
As they feel the fatal bands
Of a love they dare not name,
With a wild delicious pain,
Twine about their hearts again!
Let the early summer be
Once more round them, and the sea
Blue, and o'er its mirror kind
Let the breath of the May-wind,
Wandering through their drooping sails,
Die on the green fields of Wales!
Let a dream like this restore
What his eye must see no more!

Tristram

Chill blows the wind, the pleasaunce-walks are drear—
Madcap, what jest was this, to meet me here?
Were feet like those made for so wild a way?

The southern winter-parlour, by my fay,
Had been the likeliest trysting-place to-day!
" *Tristram !—nay, nay—thou must not take my hand !—*
Tristram !—sweet love !—we are betray'd—out-plann'd.
Fly—save thyself—save me !—I dare not stay."—
One last kiss first !—" *'Tis vain—to horse—away !"*

     *   *   *   *

Ah ! sweet saints, his dream doth move
Faster surely than it should,
From the fever in his blood !
All the spring-time of his love
Is already gone and past,
And instead thereof is seen
Its winter, which endureth still—
Tyntagel on its surge-beat hill,
The pleasaunce-walks, the weeping queen,
The flying leaves, the straining blast,
And that long, wild kiss—their last.
And this rough December-night,
And his burning fever-pain,
Mingle with his hurrying dream,
Till they rule it, till he seem
The press'd fugitive again,
The love-desperate banish'd knight
With a fire in his brain
Flying o'er the stormy main.
—Whither does he wander now ?
Haply in his dreams the wind
Wafts him here, and lets him find
The lovely orphan child again
In her castle by the coast ;
The youngest, fairest chatelaine,

Whom this realm of France can boast,
Our snowdrop by the Atlantic sea,
Iseult of Brittany.
And—for through the haggard air,
The stain'd arms, the matted hair
Of that stranger-knight ill-starr'd,
There gleam'd something, which recall'd
The Tristram who in better days
Was Launcelot's guest at Joyous Gard—
Welcomed here, and here install'd,
Tended of his fever here,
Haply he seems again to move
His young guardian's heart with love ;
In his exiled loneliness,
In his stately, deep distress,
Without a word, without a tear.
—Ah ! 'tis well he should retrace
His tranquil life in this lone place ;
His gentle bearing at the side
Of his timid youthful bride ;
His long rambles by the shore
On winter-evenings, when the roar
Of the near waves came, sadly grand,
Through the dark, up the drown'd sand,
Or his endless reveries
In the woods, where the gleams play
.On the grass under the trees,
Passing the long summer's day
Idle as a mossy stone
In the forest-depths alone,
The chase neglected, and his hound
Couch'd beside him on the ground.
—Ah ! what trouble 's on his brow ?

Hither let him wander now;
Hither, to the quiet hours
Pass'd among these heaths of ours
By the grey Atlantic sea;
Hours, if not of ecstasy,
From violent anguish surely free!

Tristram

All red with blood the whirling river flows,
The wide plain rings, the dazed air throbs with blows.
Upon us are the chivalry of Rome—
Their spears are down, their steeds are bathed in foam.
"Up, Tristram, up," men cry, "thou moonstruck knight!
What foul fiend rides thee? On into the fight!"
—Above the din her voice is in my ears;
I see her form glide through the crossing spears.—
Iseult! . . . .

*　　*　　*　　*

Ah! he wanders forth again;
We cannot keep him; now, as then,
There 's a secret in his breast
Which will never let him rest.
These musing fits in the green wood
They cloud the brain, they dull the blood!
—His sword is sharp, his horse is good;
Beyond the mountains will he see
The famous towns of Italy,
And label with the blessed sign
The heathen Saxons on the Rhine.
At Arthur's side he fights once more
With the Roman Emperor.

There's many a gay knight where he goes
Will help him to forget his care;
The march, the leaguer, Heaven's blithe air,
The neighing steeds, the ringing blows—
Sick pining comes not where these are.
Ah! what boots it, that the jest
Lightens every other brow,
What, that every other breast
Dances as the trumpets blow,
If one's own heart beats not light
On the waves of the toss'd fight,
If oneself cannot get free
From the clog of misery?
Thy lovely youthful wife grows pale
Watching by the salt sea-tide
With her children at her side
For the gleam of thy white sail.
Home, Tristram, to thy halls again!
To our lonely sea complain,
To our forests tell thy pain!

Tristram

All round the forest sweeps off, black in shade,
But it is moonlight in the open glade;
And in the bottom of the glade shine clear
The forest-chapel and the fountain near.
—I think, I have a fever in my blood;
Come, let me leave the shadow of this wood,
Ride down, and bathe my hot brow in the flood.
—Mild shines the cold spring in the moon's clear light;
God! 'tis *her* face plays in the waters bright.
"Fair love," she says, "canst thou forget so soon,

At this soft hour, under this sweet moon ? " —
Iseult ! . . .

   *   *   *   *

  Ah, poor soul ! if this be so,
  Only death can balm thy woe.
  The solitudes of the green wood
  Had no medicine for thy mood ;
  The rushing battle clear'd thy blood
  As little as did solitude.
  —Ah ! his eyelids slowly break
  Their hot seals, and let him wake ;
  What new change shall we now see ?
  A happier ? Worse it cannot be.

Tristram

Is my page here ? Come, turn me to the fire !
Upon the window-panes the moon shines bright ;
The wind is down—but she'll not come to-night.
Ah no ! she is asleep in Cornwall now,
Far hence ; her dreams are fair—smooth is her brow
Of me she recks not, nor my vain desire.
—I have had dreams, I have had dreams, my page,
Would take a score years from a strong man's age ;
And with a blood like mine, will leave, I fear,
Scant leisure for a second messenger.
—My princess, art thou there ? Sweet, do not wait !
To bed, and sleep ! my fever is gone by ;
To-night my page shall keep me company.
Where do the children sleep ? kiss them for me !
Poor child, thou art almost as pale as I ;
This comes of nursing long and watching late.
To bed—good night !

   *   *   *   *

She left the gleam-lit fireplace,
She came to the bed-side;
She took his hands in hers—her tears
Down on his wasted fingers rain'd.
She raised her eyes upon his face—
Not with a look of wounded pride,
A look as if the heart complained—
Her look was like a sad embrace;
The gaze of one who can divine
A grief, and sympathise.
Sweet flower! thy children's eyes
Are not more innocent than thine.

But they sleep in shelter'd rest,
Like helpless birds in the warm nest,
On the castle's southern side;
Where feebly comes the mournful roar
Of buffeting wind and surging tide
Through many a room and corridor.
—Full on their window the moon's ray
Makes their chamber as bright as day.
It shines upon the blank white walls,
And on the snowy pillow falls,
And on two angel-heads doth play
Turn'd to each other—the eyes closed,
The lashes on the cheeks reposed.
Round each sweet brow the cap close-set
Hardly lets peep the golden hair;
Through the soft-open'd lips the air
Scarcely moves the coverlet.
One little wandering arm is thrown
At random on the counterpane,
And often the fingers close in haste
As if their baby-owner chased

The butterflies again.
This stir they have, and this alone;
But else they are so still!
—Ah, tired madcaps! you lie still;
But were you at the window now,
To look forth on the fairy sight
Of your illumined haunts by night,
To see the park-glades where you play
Far lovelier than they are by day,
To see the sparkle on the eaves,
And upon every giant-bough
Of those old oaks, whose wet red leaves
Are jewell'd with bright drops of rain—
How would your voices run again!
And far beyond the sparkling trees
Of the castle-park one sees
The bare heaths spreading, clear as day,
Moor behind moor, far, far away,
Into the heart of Brittany.
And here and there, lock'd by the land,
Long inlets of smooth glittering sea,
And many a stretch of watery sand
All shining in the white moon-beams—
But you see fairer in your dreams!

What voices are these on the clear night-air?
What lights in the court—what steps on the stair?

II
Iseult of Ireland

Tristram

RAISE the light, my page! that I may see her.—
Thou art come at last, then, haughty Queen!

Long I've waited, long I've fought my fever,
Late thou comest, cruel thou hast been.

Iseult

Blame me not, poor sufferer! that I tarried;
Bound I was, I could not break the band.
Chide not with the past, but feel the present!
I am here—we meet—I hold thy hand.

Tristram

Thou art come, indeed—thou hast rejoin'd me;
Thou hast dared it—but too late to save.
Fear not now that men should tax thine honour!
I am dying : build—(thou may'st)—my grave!

Iseult

Tristram, ah, for love of Heaven, speak kindly!
What, I hear these bitter words from thee?
Sick with grief I am, and faint with travel—
Take my hand—dear Tristram, look on me!

Tristram

I forgot, thou comest from thy voyage—
Yes, the spray is on thy cloak and hair.
But thy dark eyes are not dimm'd, proud Iseult!
And thy beauty never was more fair.

Iseult

Ah, harsh flatterer! let alone my beauty!
I, like thee, have left my youth afar.
Take my hand, and touch these wasted fingers—
See my cheek and lips, how white they are!

Tristram

Thou art paler—but thy sweet charm, Iseult!
  Would not fade with the dull years away.
Ah, how fair thou standest in the moonlight!
  I forgive thee, Iseult!—thou wilt stay?

Iseult

Fear me not, I will be always with thee;
  I will watch thee, tend thee, soothe thy pain;
Sing thee tales of true, long-parted lovers,
  Join'd at evening of their days again.

Tristram

No, thou shalt not speak! I should be finding
  Something alter'd in thy courtly tone.
Sit—sit by me! I will think, we've lived so
  In the green wood, all our lives, alone.

Iseult

Alter'd, Tristram?   Not in courts, believe me,
  Love like mine is alter'd in the breast;
Courtly life is light and cannot reach it—
  Ah! it lives, because so deep-suppress'd!

What, thou think'st men speak in courtly chambers
  Words by which the wretched are consoled?
What, thou think'st this aching brow was cooler,
  Circled, Tristram, by a band of gold?

Royal state with Marc, my deep-wrong'd husband—
  That was bliss to make my sorrows flee!
Silken courtiers whispering honied nothings—
  Those were friends to make me false to thee!

Ah, on which, if both our lots were balanced,
  Was indeed the heaviest burden thrown—
Thee, a pining exile in thy forest,
  Me, a smiling queen upon my throne?

Vain and strange debate, where both have suffer'd
  Both have pass'd a youth consumed and sad,
Both have brought their anxious day to evening,
  And have now short space for being glad!

Join'd we are henceforth; nor will thy people,
  Nor thy younger Iseult take it ill,
That a former rival shares her office,
  When she sees her humbled, pale, and still.

I, a faded watcher by thy pillow,
  I, a statue on thy chapel-floor,
Pour'd in prayer before the Virgin-Mother,
  Rouse no anger, make no rivals more.

She will cry: "Is this the foe I dreaded?
  This his idol? this that royal bride?
Ah, an hour of health would purge his eyesight!
  Stay, pale queen! for ever by my side."

Hush, no words! that smile, I see, forgives me.
  I am now thy nurse, I bid thee sleep.
Close thine eyes — this flooding moonlight blinds
      them !—
  Nay, all's well again! thou must not weep.

Tristram

I am happy! yet I feel, there's something
  Swells my heart, and takes my breath away.
Through a mist I see thee; near—come nearer!
  Bend—bend down!—I yet have much to say.

Iseult

Heaven! his head sinks back upon the pillow—
Tristram! Tristram! let thy heart not fail!
Call on God and on the holy angels!
    What, love, courage!—Christ! he is so pale.

Tristram

Hush, 'tis vain, I feel my end approaching!
    This is what my mother said should be,
When the fierce pains took her in the forest,
    The deep draughts of death, in bearing me.

"Son," she said, "thy name shall be of sorrow;
    Tristram art thou call'd for my death's sake."
So she said, and died in the drear forest.
    Grief since then his home with me doth make.

I am dying.—Start not, nor look wildly!
    Me, thy living friend, thou canst not save.
But, since living we were ununited,
    Go not far, O Iseult! from my grave.

Close mine eyes, then seek the princess Iseult;
    Speak her fair, she is of royal blood!
Say, I will'd so, that thou stay beside me—
    She will grant it; she is kind and good.

Now to sail the seas of death I leave thee—
    One last kiss upon the living shore!

Iseult

Tristram!—Tristram!—stay—receive me with thee!
Iseult leaves thee, Tristram! never more.

    *   *   *   *

You see them clear—the moon shines bright.
Slow, slow and softly, where she stood,
She sinks upon the ground ;—her hood
Had fallen back ; her arms outspread
Still hold her lover's hand ; her head
Is bow'd, half-buried, on the bed.
O'er the blanch'd sheet her raven hair
Lies in disorder'd streams ; and there,
Strung like white stars, the pearls still are,
And the golden bracelets, heavy and rare,
Flash on her white arms still.
The very same which yesternight
Flash'd in the silver sconces' light,
When the feast was gay and the laughter loud
In Tyntagel's palace proud.
But then they deck'd a restless ghost
With hot-flush'd cheeks and brilliant eyes,
And quivering lips on which the tide
Of courtly speech abruptly died,
And a glance which over the crowded floor,
The dancers, and the festive host, .
Flew ever to the door.
That the knights eyed her in surprise,
And the dames whispered scoffingly :
" Her moods, good lack, they pass like showers !
But yesternight and she would be
As pale and still as wither'd flowers,
And now to-night she laughs and speaks
And has a colour in her cheeks ;
Christ keep us from such fantasy !"—

Yes, now the longing is o'erpast,
Which, dogg'd by fear and fought by shame,

Shook her weak bosom day and night,
Consumed her beauty like a flame,
And dimm'd it like the desert-blast.
And though the bed-clothes hide her face,
Yet were it lifted to the light,
The sweet expression of her brow
Would charm the gazer, till his thought
Erased the ravages of time,
Fill'd up the hollow cheek, and brought
A freshness back as of her prime—
So healing is her quiet now.
So perfectly the lines express
A tranquil, settled loveliness,
Her younger rival's purest grace.

The air of the December-night
Steals coldly around the chamber bright,
Where those lifeless lovers be ;
Swinging with it, in the light
Flaps the ghostlike tapestry.
And on the arras wrought you see
A stately Huntsman, clad in green,
And round him a fresh forest-scene.
On that clear forest-knoll he stays,
With his pack round him, and delays.
He stares and stares, with troubled face,
At this huge, gleam-lit fireplace,
At that bright, iron-figured door,
And those blown rushes on the floor.
He gazes down into the room
With heated cheeks and flurried air,
And to himself he seems to say :
" *What place is this, and who are they ?*

Who is that kneeling Lady fair ?
And on his pillows that pale Knight
Who seems of marble on a tomb ?
How comes it here, this chamber bright,
Through whose mullion'd windows clear
The castle-court all wet with rain,
The drawbridge and the moat appear,
And then the beach, and, mark'd with spray,
The sunken reefs, and far away
The unquiet bright Atlantic plain ?
—What, has some glamour made me sleep,
And sent me with my dogs to sweep,
By night, with boisterous bugle-peal,
Through some old, sea-side, knightly hall,
Not in the free green wood at all ?
That Knight's asleep, and at her prayer
That Lady by the bed doth kneel—
Then hush, thou boisterous bugle-peal ! "
—The wild boar rustles in his lair ;
The fierce hounds snuff the tainted air ;
But lord and hounds keep rooted there.

Cheer, cheer thy dogs into the brake,
O Hunter ! and without a fear
Thy golden-tassell'd bugle blow,
And through the glades thy pastime take—
For thou wilt rouse no sleepers here !
For these thou seest are unmoved ;
Cold, cold as those who lived and loved
A thousand years ago.

III

Iseult of Brittany

A YEAR had flown, and o'er the sea away,
In Cornwall, Tristram and Queen Iseult lay;
In King Marc's chapel, in Tyntagel old—
There in a ship they bore those lovers cold.

The young surviving Iseult, one bright day,
Had wander'd forth.   Her children were at play
In a green circular hollow in the heath
Which borders the sea-shore—a country path
Creeps over it from the till'd fields behind.
The hollow's grassy banks are soft-inclined,
And to one standing on them, far and near
The lone unbroken view spreads bright and clear
Over the waste.   This cirque of open ground
Is light and green; the heather, which all round
Creeps thickly, grows not here; but the pale grass
Is strewn with rocks, and many a shiver'd mass
Of vein'd white-gleaming quartz, and here and there
Dotted with holly-trees and juniper.
In the smooth centre of the opening stood
Three hollies side by side, and made a screen,
Warm with the winter-sun, of burnish'd green
With scarlet berries gemm'd, the fell-fare's food.
Under the glittering hollies Iseult stands,
Watching her children play; their little hands
Are busy gathering spars of quartz, and streams
Of stagshorn for their hats; anon, with screams
Of mad delight they drop their spoils, and bound
Among the holly-clumps and broken ground,
Racing full speed, and startling in their rush

The fell-fares and the speckled missel-thrush
Out of their glossy coverts ;—but when now
Their cheeks were flush'd, and over each hot brow,
Under the feather'd hats of the sweet pair,
In blinding masses shower'd the golden hair—
Then Iseult call'd them to her, and the three
Cluster'd under the holly-screen, and she
Told them an old-world Breton history.

Warm in their mantles wrapt the three stood there,
Under the hollies, in the clear still air—
Mantles with those rich furs deep glistering
Which Venice ships do from swart Egypt bring.
Long they stay'd still—then, pacing at their ease,
Moved up and down under the glossy trees.
But still, as they pursued their warm dry road,
From Iseult's lips the unbroken story flow'd,
And still the children listen'd, their blue eyes
Fix'd on their mother's face in wide surprise ;
Nor did their looks stray once to the sea-side,
Nor to the brown heaths round them, bright and wide,
Nor to the snow, which, though 't was all away
From the open heath, still by the hedgerows lay,
Nor to the shining sea-fowl, that with screams
Bore up from where the bright Atlantic gleams,
Swooping to landward ; nor to where, quite clear,
The fell-fares settled on the thickets near.
And they would still have listen'd, till dark night
Came keen and chill down on the heather bright ;
But, when the red glow on the sea grew cold,
And the grey turrets of the castle old
Look'd sternly through the frosty evening-air,
Then Iseult took by the hand those children fair,

And brought her tale to an end, and found the path,
And led them home over the darkening heath.

And is she happy? Does she see unmoved
The days in which she might have lived and loved
Slip without bringing bliss slowly away,
One after one, to-morrow like to-day?
Joy has not found her yet, nor ever will—
Is it this thought which makes her mien so still,
Her features so fatigued, her eyes, though sweet,
So sunk, so rarely lifted save to meet
Her children's? She moves slow; her voice alone
Hath yet an infantine and silver tone,
But even that comes languidly; in truth,
She seems one dying in a mask of youth.
And now she will go home, and softly lay
Her laughing children in their beds, and play
Awhile with them before they sleep; and then
She'll light her silver lamp, which fishermen
Dragging their nets through the rough waves, afar,
Along this iron coast, know like a star,
And take her broidery-frame, and there she'll sit
Hour after hour, her gold curls sweeping it;
Lifting her soft-bent head only to mind
Her children, or to listen to the wind.
And when the clock peals midnight, she will move
Her work away, and let her fingers rove
Across the shaggy brows of Tristram's hound
Who lies, guarding her feet, along the ground;
Or else she will fall musing, her blue eyes
Fixt, her slight hands clasp'd on her lap; then rise,
And at her prie-dieu kneel, until she have told
Her rosary-beads of ebony tipp'd with gold,

Then to her soft sleep—and to-morrow 'll be
To-day's exact repeated effigy.

Yes, it is lonely for her in her hall.
The children, and the grey-hair'd seneschal,
Her women, and Sir Tristram's aged hound,
Are there the sole companions to be found.
But these she loves; and noisier life than this
She would find ill to bear, weak as she is.
She has her children, too, and night and day
Is with them; and the wide heaths where they play,
The hollies, and the cliff, and the sea-shore,
The sand, the sea-birds, and the distant sails,
These are to her dear as to them; the tales
With which this day the children she beguiled
She gleaned from Breton grandames, when a child,
In every hut along this sea-coast wild.
She herself loves them still, and, when they are told,
Can forget all to hear them, as of old.

Dear saints, it is not sorrow, as I hear,
Not suffering, which shuts up eye and ear
To all that has delighted them before,
And lets us be what we were once no more.
No, we may suffer deeply, yet retain
Power to be moved and soothed, for all our pain,
By what of old pleased us, and will again.
No, 'tis the gradual furnace of the world,
In whose hot air our spirits are upcurl'd
Until they crumble, or else grow like steel—
Which kills in us the bloom, the youth, the spring—
Which leaves the fierce necessity to feel,
But takes away the power—this can avail,
By drying up our joy in everything,

To make our former pleasures all seem stale.
This, or some tyrannous single thought, some fit
Of passion, which subdues our souls to it,
Till for its sake alone we live and move—
Call it ambition, or remorse, or love—
This too can change us wholly, and make seem
All which we did before, shadow and dream.

And yet, I swear, it angers me to see
How this fool passion gulls men potently;
Being, in truth, but a diseased unrest,
And an unnatural overheat at best.
How they are full of languor and distress
Not having it; which when they do possess,
They straightway are burnt up with fume and care,
And spend their lives in posting here and there
Where this plague drives them; and have little ease,
Are furious with themselves, and hard to please.
Like that bold Cæsar, the famed Roman wight,
Who wept at reading of a Grecian knight
Who made a name at younger years than he;
Or that renown'd mirror of chivalry,
Prince Alexander, Philip's peerless son,
Who carried the great war from Macedon
Into the Soudan's realm, and thundered on
To die at thirty-five in Babylon.

What tale did Iseult to the children say,
Under the hollies, that bright winter's day?

She told them of the fairy-haunted land
Away the other side of Brittany,
Beyond the heaths, edged by the lonely sea;
Of the deep forest-glades of Broce-liande,

Through whose green boughs the golden sunshine creeps,
Where Merlin by the enchanted thorn-tree sleeps.
For here he came with the fay Vivian,
One April, when the warm days first began.
He was on foot, and that false fay, his friend,
On her white palfrey ; here he met his end,
In these lone sylvan glades, that April-day.
This tale of Merlin and the lovely fay
Was the one Iseult chose, and she brought clear
Before the children's fancy him and her.

Blowing between the stems, the forest-air
Had loosen'd the brown locks of Vivian's hair,
Which play'd on her flush'd cheek, and her blue eyes
Sparkled with mocking glee and exercise.
Her palfrey's flanks were mired and bathed in sweat,
For they had travell'd far and not stopp'd yet.
A brier in that tangled wilderness
Had scored her white right hand, which she allows
To rest ungloved on her green riding-dress ;
The other warded off the drooping boughs.
But still she chatted on, with her blue eyes
Fix'd full on Merlin's face, her stately prize.
Her 'haviour had the morning's fresh clear grace,
The spirit of the woods was in her face.
She look'd so witching fair, that learned wight
Forgot his craft, and his best wits took flight ;
And he grew fond, and eager to obey
His mistress, use her empire as she may.

They came to where the brushwood ceased, and day
Peer'd 'twixt the stems ; and the ground broke away,
In a sloped sward down to a brawling brook ;
And up as high as where they stood to look

On the brook's farther side was clear, but then
The underwood and trees began again.
This open glen was studded thick with thorns
Then white with blossom ; and you saw the horns,
Through last year's fern, of the shy fallow-deer
Who come at noon down to the water here.
You saw the bright-eyed squirrels dart along
Under the thorns on the green sward ; and strong
The blackbird whistled from the dingles near,
And the weird chipping of the woodpecker
Rang lonelily and sharp ; the sky was fair,
And a fresh breath of spring stirr'd everywhere.
Merlin and Vivian stopp'd on the slope's brow,
To gaze on the light sea of leaf and bough
Which glistering plays all round them, lone and mild,
As if to itself the quiet forest smiled.
Upon the brow-top grew a thorn, and here
The grass was dry and moss'd, and you saw clear
Across the hollow ; white anemonies
Starr'd the cool turf, and clumps of primroses
Ran out from the dark underwood behind.
No fairer resting-place a man could find.
"Here let us halt," said Merlin then ; and she
Nodded, and tied her palfrey to a tree.

They sate them down together, and a sleep
Fell upon Merlin, more like death, so deep.
Her finger on her lips, then Vivian rose,
And from her brown-lock'd head the wimple throws,
And takes it in her hand, and waves it over
The blossom'd thorn-tree and her sleeping lover.
Nine times she waved the fluttering wimple round,
And made a little plot of magic ground.

And in that daised circle, as men say,
Is Merlin prisoner till the judgment-day ;
But she herself whither she will can rove—
For she was passing weary of his love.

THE DEFENCE OF GUENEVERE

BUT, knowing now that they would have her speak,
She threw her wet hair backward from her brow,
Her hand close to her mouth touching her cheek,

As though she had had there a shameful blow,
And feeling it shameful to feel ought but shame
All through her heart, yet felt her cheek burned so,

She must a little touch it; like one lame
She walked away from Gauwaine, with her head
Still lifted up; and on her cheek of flame

The tears dried quick; she stopped at last and said:
"O knights and lords, it seems but little skill
To talk of well-known things past now and dead.

"God wot I ought to say, I have done ill,
And pray you all forgiveness heartily!
Because you must be right such great lords—still *- pandering / sarcasm*

"Listen, suppose your time were come to die,
And you were quite alone and very weak;
Yea, laid a dying while very mightily

"The wind was ruffling up the narrow streak
Of river through your broad lands running well:
Suppose a hush should come, then some one speak:

"'One of these cloths is heaven, and one is hell,
Now choose one cloth for ever, which they be,
I will not tell you, you must somehow tell

"'Of your own strength and mightiness; here, see!'
Yea, yea, my lord, and you to ope your eyes,
At foot of your familiar bed to see

"A great God's angel standing, with such dyes,
Not known on earth, on his great wings, and hands,
Held out two ways, light from the inner skies

"Showing him well, and making his commands
Seem to be God's commands, moreover, too,
Holding within his hands the cloths on wands;

"And one of these strange choosing cloths was blue,
Wavy and long, and one cut short and red;
No man could tell the better of the two.

"After a shivering half-hour you said,
'God help! heaven's colour, the blue;' and he said, 'hell.'
Perhaps you then would roll upon your bed,

"And cry to all good men that loved you well,
'Ah Christ! if only I had known, known, known;'
Launcelot went away, then I could tell,

"Like wisest man how all things would be, moan,
And roll and hurt myself, and long to die,
And yet fear much to die for what was sown.

"Nevertheless you, O Sir Gauwaine, lie,   *refrain*
Whatever may have happened through these years,
God knows I speak truth, saying that you lie."

Her voice was low at first, being full of tears,
But as it cleared, it grew full loud and shrill,
Growing a windy shriek in all men's ears,

A ringing in their startled brains, until
She said that Gauwaine lied, then her voice sunk,
And her great eyes began again to fill,

Though still she stood right up, and never shrunk,
But spoke on bravely, glorious lady fair!
Whatever tears her full lips may have drunk,

She stood, and seemed to think, and wrung her hair,
Spoke out at last with no more trace of shame,
With passionate twisting of her body there:

" It chanced upon a day that Launcelot came
To dwell at Arthur's court : at Christmas-time
This happened; when the heralds sung his name,

" 'Son of King Ban of Benwick,' seemed to chime
Along with all the bells that rang that day,
O'er the white roofs, with little change of rhyme.

" Christmas and whitened winter passed away,
And over me the April sunshine came,
Made very awful with black hail-clouds, yea

" And in the Summer I grew white with flame,
And bowed my head down—Autumn, and the sick
Sure knowledge things would never be the same,

" However often Spring might be most thick
Of blossoms and buds, smote on me, and I grew
Careless of most things, let the clock tick, tick,

" To my unhappy pulse, that beat right through
My eager body ; while I laughed out loud,
And let my lips curl up at false or true,

" Seemed cold and shallow without any cloud.
Behold my judges, then the cloths were brought :
While I was dizzied thus, old thoughts would crowd,

" Belonging to the time ere I was bought
By Arthur's great name and his little love,
Must I give up for ever then, I thought,

" That which I deemed would ever round me move
Glorifying all things ; for a little word,
Scarce ever meant at all, must I now prove

" Stone-cold for ever?   Pray you, does the Lord
Will that all folks should be quite happy and good?
I love God now a little, if this cord

" Were broken, once for all what striving could
Make me love anything in earth or heaven.
So day by day it grew, as if one should

" Slip slowly down some path worn smooth and even,
Down to a cool sea on a summer day ;
Yet still in slipping was there some small leaven

"Of stretched hands catching small stones by the way,
Until one surely reached the sea at last,
And felt strange new joy as the worn head lay

"Back, with the hair like sea-weed; yea all past
Sweat of the forehead, dryness of the lips,
Washed utterly out by the dear waves o'ercast

"In the lone sea, far off from any ships!
Do I not know now of a day in Spring?
No minute of that wild day ever slips

"From out my memory; I hear thrushes sing,
And wheresoever I may be, straightway
Thoughts of it all come up with most fresh sting;

"I was half mad with beauty on that day,
And went without my ladies all alone,
In a quiet garden walled round every way;

"I was right joyful of that wall of stone,
That shut the flowers and trees up with the sky,
And trebled all the beauty: to the bone,

"Yea right through to my heart, grown very shy
With weary thoughts, it pierced, and made me glad;
Exceedingly glad, and I knew verily,

"A little thing just then had made me mad;
I dared not think, as I was wont to do,
Sometimes, upon my beauty; if I had

"Held out my long hand up against the blue,
And, looking on the tenderly darken'd fingers,
Thought that by rights one ought to see quite through,

"There, see you, where the soft still light yet lingers,
Round by the edges; what should I have done,
If this had joined with yellow spotted singers,

"And startling green drawn upward by the sun?
But shouting, loosed out, see now! all my hair,
And trancedly stood watching the west wind run

"With faintest half-heard breathing sound—why there
I lose my head e'en now in doing this;
But shortly listen—In that garden fair

" Came Launcelot walking; this is true, the kiss
Wherewith we kissed in meeting that spring day,
I scarce dare talk of the remember'd bliss,

" When both our mouths went wandering in one way,
And aching sorely, met among the leaves;
Our hands being left behind strained far away.

" Never within a yard of my bright sleeves
Had Launcelot come before—and now, so nigh!
After that day why is it Guenevere grieves?

" Nevertheless you, O Sir Gauwaine, lie,   refrain
Whatever happened on through all those years,
God knows I speak truth, saying that you lie.

" Being such a lady could I weep these tears
If this were true?   A great queen such as I
Having sinn'd this way, straight her conscience sears;

" And afterwards she liveth hatefully,
Slaying and poisoning, certes never weeps,—
Gauwaine be friends now, speak me lovingly.

" Do I not see how God's dear pity creeps
All through your frame, and trembles in your mouth?
Remember in what grave your mother sleeps,

" Buried in some place far down in the south,
Men are forgetting as I speak to you;
By her head sever'd in that awful drouth

" Of pity that drew Agravaine's fell blow,
I pray your pity! let me not scream out
For ever after, when the shrill winds blow

" Through half your castle-locks! let me not shout
For ever after in the winter night
When you ride out alone! in battle-rout

" Let not my rusting tears make your sword light!
Ah! God of mercy how he turns away!
So, ever must I dress me to the fight,

" So—let God's justice work! Gauwaine, I say,
See me hew down your proofs: yea all men know
Even as you said how Mellyagraunce one day,

" One bitter day in *la Fausse Garde*, for so
All good knights held it after, saw—
Yea, sirs, by cursed unknightly outrage; though

"You, Gauwaine, held his word without a flaw,
This Mellyagraunce saw blood upon my bed—
Whose blood then pray you? is there any law

"To make a queen say why some spots of red
Lie on her coverlet? or will you say,
'Your hands are white, lady, as when you wed,

"'Where did you bleed?' and must I stammer out—'Nay,
I blush indeed, fair lord, only to rend
My sleeve up to my shoulder, where there lay

"'A knife-point last night:' so must I defend
The honour of the Lady Guenevere?
Not so, fair lords, even if the world should end

"This very day, and you were judges here
Instead of God.   Did you see Mellyagraunce
When Launcelot stood by him? what white fear

"Curdled his blood, and how his teeth did dance
His side sink in? as my knight cried and said,
'Slayer of unarm'd men, here is a chance!

"'Setter of traps, I pray you guard your head,
By God I am so glad to fight with you,
Stripper of ladies, that my hand feels lead

"'For driving weight; hurrah now! draw and do,
For all my wounds are moving in my breast,
And I am getting mad with waiting so.'

" He struck his hands together o'er the beast,
Who fell down flat, and grovell'd at his feet,
And groan'd at being slain so young—'at least.'

" My knight said, 'Rise you, sir, who are so fleet
At catching ladies, half-arm'd will I fight,
My left side all uncovered ! ' then I weet.

" Up sprang Sir Mellyagraunce with great delight
Upon his knave's face; not until just then
Did I quite hate him, as I saw my knight

" Along the lists look to my stake and pen
With such a joyous smile, it made me sigh
From agony beneath my waist-chain, when

" The fight began, and to me they drew nigh ;
Ever Sir Launcelot kept him on the right,
And traversed warily, and ever high

" And fast leapt caitiff's sword, until my knight
Sudden threw up his sword to his left hand,
Caught it, and swung it ; that was all the fight.

" Except a spout of blood on the hot land ;
For it was hottest summer ; and I know
I wonder'd how the fire, while I should stand,

" And burn, against the heat, would quiver so,
Yards above my head ; thus these matters went ;
Which things were only warnings of the woe

" That fell on me.   Yet Mellyagraunce was shent,
For Mellyagraunce had fought against the Lord ;
Therefore, my lords, take heed lest you be blent

" With all this wickedness ; say no rash word
Against me, being so beautiful ; my eyes,
Wept all away to grey, may bring some sword

" To drown you in your blood ; see my breast rise,
Like waves of purple sea, as here I stand ;
And how my arms are moved in wonderful wise,

" Yea also at my full heart's strong command,
See through my long throat how the words go up
In ripples to my mouth ; how in my hand

" The shadow lies like wine within a cup
Of marvellously colour'd gold ; yea now
This little wind is rising, look you up,

" And wonder how the light is falling so
Within my moving tresses : will you dare,
When you have looked a little on my brow,

" To say this thing is vile ? or will you care
For any plausible lies of cunning woof,
When you can see my face with no lie there

" For ever? am I not a gracious proof—
' But in your chamber Launcelot was found '—
Is there a good knight then would stand aloof,

" When a queen says with gentle queenly sound:
' O true as steel come now and talk with me,
I love to see your step upon the ground

" ' Unwavering, also well I love to see
That gracious smile light up your face, and hear
Your wonderful words, that all mean verily

" ' The thing they seem to mean: good friend, so dear
To me in everything, come here to-night,
Or else the hours will pass most dull and drear;

" ' If you come not, I fear this time I might
Get thinking over much of times gone by,
When I was young, and green hope was in sight;

" ' For no man cares now to know why I sigh;
And no man comes to sing me pleasant songs,
Nor any brings me the sweet flowers that lie

" ' So thick in the gardens; therefore one so longs
To see you, Launcelot; that we may be
Like children once again, free from all wrongs

" ' Just for one night.' Did he not come to me?
What thing could keep true Launcelot away
If I said ' come '? there was one less than three

" In my quiet room that night, and we were gay;
Till sudden I rose up, weak, pale, and sick,
Because a bawling broke our dream up, yea

" I looked at Launcelot's face and could not speak,
For he looked helpless too, for a little while;
Then I remember how I tried to shriek,

" And could not, but fell down; from tile to tile
The stones they threw up rattled o'er my head,
And made me dizzier; till within a while

" My maids were all about me, and my head
On Launcelot's breast was being soothed away
From its white chattering, until Launcelot said—

" By God! I will not tell you more to-day,
Judge any way you will—what matters it?
You know quite well the story of that fray,

" How Launcelot still'd their bawling, the mad fit
That caught up Gauwaine—all, all, verily,
But just that which would save me; these things flit.

" Nevertheless you, O Sir Gauwaine, lie,
Whatever may have happen'd these long years,
God knows I speak truth, saying that you lie!

" All I have said is truth, by Christ's dear tears."
She would not speak another word, but stood
Turn'd sideways; listening, like a man who hears

His brother's trumpet sounding through the wood
Of his foes' lances. She lean'd eagerly,
And gave a slight spring sometimes, as she could

At last hear something really; joyfully
Her cheek grew crimson, as the headlong speed
Of the roan charger drew all men to see,
The knight who came was Launcelot at good need.

KING ARTHUR'S TOMB

HOT August noon—already on that day
  Since sunrise through the Wiltshire downs, most sad
Of mouth and eye, he had gone leagues of way ;
  Ay and by night, till whether good or bad

He was, he knew not, though he knew perchance
  That he was Launcelot, the bravest knight
Of all who since the world was, have borne lance,
  Or swung their swords in wrong cause or in right.

Nay, he knew nothing now, except that where
  The Glastonbury gilded towers shine,
A lady dwelt, whose name was Guenevere ;
  This he knew also ; that some fingers twine,

Not only in a man's hair, even his heart,
  (Making him good or bad I mean,) but in his life,
Skies, earth, men's looks and deeds, all that has part,
  Not being ourselves, in that half-sleep, half-strife,

(Strange sleep, strange strife,) that men call living ; so
  Was Launcelot most glad when the moon rose,
Because it brought new memories of her—" Lo,
  Between the trees a large moon, the wind lows

" Not loud, but as a cow begins to low,
  Wishing for strength to make the herdsman hear :
The ripe corn gathereth dew ; yea, long ago,
  In the old garden life, my Guenevere

" Loved to sit still among the flowers, till night
  Had quite come on, hair loosen'd, for she said,
Smiling like heaven, that its fairness might
  Draw up the wind sooner to cool her head.

"Now while I ride how quick the moon gets small,
    As it did then—I tell myself a tale
That will not last beyond the whitewashed wall,
    Thoughts of some joust must help me through the vale,

"Keep this till after—How Sir Gareth ran
    A good course that day under my Queen's eyes,
And how she sway'd laughing at Dinadan—
    No—back again, the other thoughts will rise,

"And yet I think so fast 'twill end right soon—
    Verily then I think, that Guenevere,
Made sad by dew and wind, and tree-barred moon,
    Did love me more than ever, was more dear

"To me than ever, she would let me lie
    And kiss her feet, or, if I sat behind,
Would drop her hand and arm most tenderly,
    And touch my mouth.   And she would let me wind

"Her hair around my neck, so that it fell
    Upon my red robe, strange in the twilight
With many unnamed colours, till the bell
    Of her mouth on my cheek sent a delight

"Through all my ways of being ; like the stroke
    Wherewith God threw all men upon the face
When he took Enoch, and when Enoch woke
    With a changed body in the happy place.

"Once, I remember, as I sat beside,
    She turn'd a little, and laid back her head,
And slept upon my breast : I almost died
    In those night-watches with my love and dread,

"There lily-like she bow'd her head and slept,
    And I breathed low, and did not dare to move,
But sat and quiver'd inwardly, thoughts crept,
    And frighten'd me with pulses of my Love.

"The stars shone out above the doubtful green
    Of her boddice, in the green sky overhead ;
Pale in the green sky were the stars I ween,
    Because the moon shone like a star she shed

" When she dwelt up in heaven a while ago,
   And ruled all things but God : the night went on,
The wind grew cold, and the white moon grew low,
   One hand had fallen down, and now lay on

" My cold stiff palm ; there were no colours then
   For near an hour, and I fell asleep
In spite of all my striving, even when
   I held her whose name-letters make me leap.

" I did not sleep long, feeling that in sleep
   I did some loved one wrong, so that the sun
Had only just arisen from the deep
   Still land of colours, when before me one

" Stood whom I knew, but scarcely dared to touch,
   She seemed to have changed so in the night ;
Moreover she held scarlet lilies, such
   As Maiden Margaret bears upon the light

" Of the great church walls, natheless did I walk
   Through the fresh wet woods, and the wheat that
      morn,
Touching her hair and hand and mouth, and talk
   Of love we held, nigh hid among the corn.

" Back to the palace, ere the sun grew high,
   We went, and in a cool green room all day
I gazed upon the arras giddily,
   Where the wind set the silken kings a-sway.

" I could not hold her hand, or see her face ;
   For which may God forgive me ! but I think,
Howsoever, that she was not in that place."
   These memories Launcelot was quick to drink ;

And when these fell, some paces past the wall,
   There rose yet others, but they wearied more,
And tasted not so sweet ; they did not fall
   So soon, but vaguely wrenched his strained heart sore

In shadowy slipping from his grasp ; these gone,
   A longing followed ; if he might but touch
That Guenevere at once ! Still night, the lone
   Grey horse's head before him vex'd him much,

In steady nodding over the grey road—
　　Still night, and night, and night, and emptied heart
Of any stories; what a dismal load
　　Time grew at last, yea, when the night did part,

And let the sun flame over all, still there
　　The horse's grey ears turn'd this way and that,
And still he watch'd them twitching in the glare
　　Of the morning sun, behind them still he sat,

Quite wearied out with all the wretched night,
　　Until about the dustiest of the day,
On the last down's brow he drew his rein in sight
　　Of the Glastonbury roofs that choke the way.

And he was now quite giddy as before,
　　When she slept by him, tired out and her hair
Was mingled with the rushes on the floor,
　　And he, being tired too, was scarce aware

Of her presence; yet as he sat and gazed,
　　A shiver ran throughout him, and his breath
Came slower, he seem'd suddenly amazed,
　　As though he had not heard of Arthur's death.

This for a moment only, presently
　　He rode on giddy still, until he reach'd
A place of apple-trees, by the thorn-tree
　　Wherefrom St. Joseph in the days past preached.

Dazed there he laid his head upon a tomb,
　　Not knowing it was Arthur's, at which sight
One of her maidens told her, " he is come,"
　　And she went forth to meet him; yet a blight

Had settled on her, all her robes were black,
　　With a long white veil only; she went slow,
As one walks to be slain, her eyes did lack
　　Half her old glory, yea, alas! the glow

Had left her face and hands; this was because
　　As she lay last night on her purple bed,
Wishing for morning, grudging every pause
　　Of the palace clocks, until that Launcelot's head

Should lie on her breast, with all her golden hair
  Each side—when suddenly the thing grew drear,
In morning twilight, when the grey downs bare
  Grew into lumps of sin to Guenevere.

At first she said no word, but lay quite still,
  Only her mouth was open, and her eyes
Gazed wretchedly about from hill to hill ;
  As though she asked, not with so much surprise

As tired disgust, what made them stand up there
  So cold and grey. After, a spasm took
Her face, and all her frame, she caught her hair,
  All her hair, in both hands, terribly she shook,

And rose till she was sitting in the bed,
  Set her teeth hard, and shut her eyes and seem'd
As though she would have torn it from her head,
  Natheless she dropp'd it, lay down, as she deem'd

It matter'd not whatever she might do—
  O Lord Christ ! pity on her ghastly face !
Those dismal hours while the cloudless blue
  Drew the sun higher—He did give her grace ;

Because at last she rose up from her bed,
  And put her raiment on, and knelt before
The blessed rood, and with her dry lips said,
  Muttering the words against the marble floor :

" Unless you pardon, what shall I do, Lord,
  But go to hell ? and there see day by day
Foul deed on deed, hear foulest word on word,
  For ever and ever, such as on the way

" To Camelot I heard once from a churl,
  That curled me up upon my jennet's neck
With bitter shame ; how then, Lord, should I curl
  For ages and for ages ? dost thou reck

" That I am beautiful, Lord, even as you
  And your dear Mother ? why did I forget
You were so beautiful, and good, and true,
  That you loved me so, Guenevere ?   O yet

" If even I go hell, I cannot choose
  But love you, Christ, yea, though I cannot keep
From loving Launcelot; O Christ! must I lose
  My own heart's love? see, though I cannot weep,

" Yet am I very sorry for my sin;
  Moreover, Christ, I cannot bear that hell,
I am most fain to love you, and to win
  A place in heaven some time—I cannot tell—

"Speak to me, Christ! I kiss, kiss, kiss your feet;
  Ah! now I weep!"—The maid said, " By the tomb
He waiteth for you, lady," coming fleet,
  Not knowing what woe filled up all the room.

So Guenevere rose and went to meet him there,
  He did not hear her coming, as he lay
On Arthur's head, till some of her long hair
  Brush'd on the new-cut stone—" Well done! to pray

" For Arthur, my dear lord, the greatest king
  That ever lived." " Guenevere! Guenevere
Do you not know me, are you gone mad? fling
  Your arms and hair about me, lest I fear

" You are not Guenevere, but some other thing."
  " Pray you forgive me, fair lord Launcelot!
I am not mad, but I am sick; they cling,
  God's curses, unto such as I am; not

" Ever again shall we twine arms and lips."
  " Yea, she is mad: thy heavy law, O Lord,
Is very tight about her now, and grips
  Her poor heart, so that no right word

" Can reach her mouth; so, Lord, forgive her now,
  That she not knowing what she does, being mad,
Kills me in this way—Guenevere, bend low
  And kiss me once! for God's love kiss me! sad

" Though your face is, you look much kinder now;
  Yea once, once for the last time kiss me, lest I die."
" Christ! my hot lips are very near his brow,
  Help me to save his soul!—Yea, verily,

" Across my husband's head, fair Launcelot !
   Fair serpent mark'd with V upon the head !
This thing we did while yet he was alive,
   Why not, O twisting knight, now he is dead ?

" Yea, shake! shake now and shiver! if you can
   Remember anything for agony,
Pray you remember how when the wind ran
   One cool spring evening through fair aspen-tree,

" And elm and oak about the palace there,
   The king came back from battle, and I stood
To meet him, with my ladies, on the stair,
   My face made beautiful with my young blood."

" Will she lie now, Lord God ? "   " Remember too,
   Wrung heart, how first before the knights there came
A royal bier, hung round with green and blue,
   About it shone great tapers with sick flame.

" And thereupon Lucius, the Emperor,
   Lay royal-robed, but stone-cold now and dead,
Not able to hold sword or sceptre more,
   But not quite grim ; because his cloven head

" Bore no marks now of Launcelot's bitter sword,
   Being by embalmers deftly solder'd up ;
So still it seem'd the face of a great lord,
   Being mended as a craftsman mends a cup.

" Also the heralds sung rejoicingly
   To their long trumpets ; ' Fallen under shield,
Here lieth Lucius, King of Italy,
   Slain by Lord Launcelot in open field.'

" Thereat the people shouted ' Launcelot ! '
   And through the spears I saw you drawing nigh,
You and Lord Arthur—nay, I saw you not,
   But rather Arthur, God would not let die,

" I hoped, these many years, he should grow great,
   And in his great arms still encircle me,
Kissing my face, half blinded with the heat
   Of king's love for the queen I used to be.

"Launcelot, Launcelot, why did he take your hand,
   When he had kissed me in his kingly way?
Saying, 'This is the knight whom all the land
   Calls Arthur's banner, sword, and shield to-day;

"'Cherish him, love.' Why did your long lips cleave
   In such strange way unto my fingers then?
So eagerly glad to kiss, so loath to leave
   When you rose up? Why among helmed men

"Could I always tell you by your long strong arms,
   And sway like an angel's in your saddle there?
Why sicken'd I so often with alarms
   Over the tilt-yard? Why were you more fair

"Than aspens in the autumn at their best?
   Why did you fill all lands with your great fame,
So that Breuse even, as he rode, fear'd lest
   At turning of the way your shield should flame?

"Was it nought then, my agony and strife?
   When as day passed by day, year after year,
I found I could not live a righteous life?
   Didst ever think that queens held their truth dear.

"O, but your lips say, 'Yea, but she was cold
   Sometimes, always uncertain as the spring;
When I was sad she would be overbold,
   Longing for kisses;' when war-bells did ring,

"The back-toll'd bells of noisy Camelot."—
   "Now, Lord God, listen! listen, Guenevere,
Though I am weak just now, I think there's not
   A man who dares to say, 'You hated her,

"'And left her moaning while you fought your fill
   In the daisied meadows;' lo you her thin hand,
That on the carven stone can not keep still,
   Because she loves me against God's command,

"Has often been quite wet with tear on tear,
   Tears Launcelot keeps somewhere, surely not
In his own heart, perhaps in Heaven, where
   He will not be these ages."—"Launcelot!

"Loud lips, wrung heart! I say, when the bells rang,
  The noisy back-toll'd bells of Camelot,
There were two spots on earth, the thrushes sang
  In the lonely gardens where my love was not,

"Where I was almost weeping; I dared not
  Weep quite in those days, lest one maid should say,
In tittering whispers; 'Where is Launcelot
  To wipe with some kerchief those tears away?'

"Another answer sharply with brows knit,
  And warning hand up, scarcely lower though,
'You speak too loud, see you, she heareth it,
  This tigress fair has claws, as I well know,

"'As Launcelot knows too, the poor knight! well-a-day!
  Why met he not with Iseult from the West,
Or, better still, Iseult of Brittany,
  Perchance indeed quite ladyless were best.'

"Alas, my maids, you loved not overmuch
  Queen Guenevere, uncertain as sunshine
In March; forgive me! for my sin being such,
  About my whole life, all my deeds did twine,

"Made me quite wicked; as I found out then,
  I think; in the lonely palace, where each morn
We went, my maids and I, to say prayers when
  They sang mass in the chapel on the lawn.

"And every morn I scarce could pray at all,
  For Launcelot's red-golden hair would play,
Instead of sunlight, on the painted wall,
  Mingled with dreams of what the priest did say;

"Grim curses out of Peter and of Paul;
  Judging of strange sins in Leviticus;
Another sort of writing on the wall,
  Scored deep across the painted heads of us.

"Christ sitting with the woman at the well,
  And Mary Magdalen repenting there,
Her dimmed eyes scorch'd and red at sight of hell
  So hardly scaped, no gold light on her hair.

" And if the priest said anything that seem'd
    To touch upon the sin they said we did,—
(This in their teeth) they look'd as if they deem'd
    That I was spying what thoughts might be hid

" Under green-cover'd bosoms, heaving quick
    Beneath quick thoughts; while they grew red with
        shame,
And gazed down at their feet—while I felt sick,
    And almost shriek'd if one should call my name.

" The thrushes sang in the lone garden there—
    But where you were the birds were scared I trow—
Clanging of arms about pavilions fair,
    Mixed with the knight's laughs; there, as I well know,

" Rode Launcelot, the king of all the band,
    And scowling Gauwaine, like the night in day,
And handsome Gareth, with his great white hand
    Curl'd round the helm-crest, ere he join'd the fray;

" And merry Dinadan with sharp dark face,
    All true knights loved to see; and in the fight
Great Tristram, and though helmed you could trace
    In all his bearing the frank noble knight;

" And by him Palomydes, helmet off,
    He fought, his face brush'd by his hair,
Red heavy swinging hair; he fear'd a scoff
    So overmuch, though what true knight would dare

" To mock that face, fretted with useless care,
    And bitter useless striving after love?
O Palomydes, with much honour bear
    Beast Glatysaunt upon your shield, above

" Your helm that hides the swinging of your hair,
    And think of Iseult, as your sword drives through
Much mail and plate—O God, let me be there
    A little time, as I was long ago!

" Because stout Gareth lets his spear fall low,
    Gauwaine, and Launcelot, and Dinadan
Are helm'd and waiting; let the trumpets go!
    Bend over, ladies, to see all you can!

"Clench teeth, dames, yea, clasp hands, for Gareth's spear
Throws Kay from out his saddle, like a stone
From a castle-window when the foe draws near—
'Iseult!'—Sir Dinadan rolleth overthrown.

"'Iseult!'—again—the pieces of each spear
Fly fathoms up, and both the great steeds reel;
'Tristram for Iseult!' 'Iseult!' and 'Guenevere,'
The ladies' names bite verily like steel.

"They bite—bite me, Lord God—I shall go mad,
Or else die kissing him, he is so pale,
He thinks me mad already, O bad! bad!
Let me lie down a little while and wail."

"No longer so, rise up, I pray you, love,
And slay me really, then we shall be heal'd,
Perchance, in the aftertime by God above."
"Banner of Arthur—with black-bended shield

"Sinister-wise across the fair gold ground!
Here let me tell you what a knight you are,
O sword and shield of Arthur! you are found
A crooked sword, I think, that leaves a scar

"On the bearer's arm, so be he thinks it straight,
Twisted Malay's crease beautiful blue-grey,
Poison'd with sweet fruit; as he found too late,
My husband Arthur, on some bitter day!

"O sickle cutting hemlock the day long!
That the husbandman across his shoulder hangs,
And, going homeward about evensong,
Dies the next morning, struck through by the fangs!

"Banner, and sword, and shield, you dare not pray to die,
Lest you meet Arthur in the other world,
And, knowing who you are, he pass you by,
Taking short turns that he may watch you curl'd

"Body and face and limbs in agony,
Lest he weep presently and go away,
Saying, 'I loved him once,' with a sad sigh—
Now I have slain him, Lord, let me go too, I pray.
[LAUNCELOT *falls.*

" Alas, alas ! I know not what to do,
  If I run fast it is perchance that I
May fall and stun myself, much better so,
  Never, never again ! not even when I die."

                    LAUNCELOT, *on awaking.*

" I stretch'd my hands towards her and fell down,
  How long I lay in swoon I cannot tell :
My head and hands were bleeding from the stone,
  When I rose up, also I heard a bell."

SIR GALAHAD,
A CHRISTMAS MYSTERY

IT is the longest night in all the year,
  Near on the day when the Lord Christ was born;
Six hours ago I came and sat down here,
  And ponder'd sadly, wearied and forlorn.

The winter wind that pass'd the chapel-door,
  Sang out a moody tune, that went right well
With mine own thoughts: I look'd down on the floor,
  Between my feet, until I heard a bell

Sound a long way off through the forest deep,
  And toll on steadily; a drowsiness
Came on me, so that I fell half asleep,
  As I sat there not moving : less and less

I saw the melted snow that hung in beads
  Upon my steel-shoes; less and less I saw
Between the tiles the bunches of small weeds:
  Heartless and stupid, with no touch of awe

Upon me, half-shut eyes upon the ground,
  I thought; O! Galahad, the days go by,
Stop and cast up now that which you have found,
  So sorely you have wrought and painfully.

Night after night your horse treads down alone
  The sere damp fern, night after night you sit
Holding the bridle like a man of stone,
  Dismal, unfriended, what thing comes of it.

And what if Palomydes also ride,
  And over many a mountain and bare heath
Follow the questing beast with none beside?
  Is he not able still to hold his breath

With thoughts of Iseult? doth he not grow pale
  With weary striving, to seem best of all
To her, " as she is best," he saith? to fail
  Is nothing to him, he can never fall.

For unto such a man love-sorrow is
  So dear a thing unto his constant heart,
That even if he never win one kiss,
  Or touch from Iseult, it will never part.

And he will never know her to be worse
  Than in his happiest dreams he thinks she is :
Good knight, and faithful, you have 'scaped the curse
  In wonderful-wise; you have great store of bliss.

Yea, what if Father Launcelot ride out,
  Can he not think of Guenevere's arms, round,
Warm and lithe, about his neck, and shout
  Till all the place grows joyful with the sound?

And when he lists can often see her face,
  And think, " Next month I kiss you, or next week,
And still you think of me : " therefore the place
  Grows very pleasant, whatsoever he seek.

But me, who ride alone, some carle shall find
  Dead in my arms in the half-melted snow,
When all unkindly with the shifting wind,
  The thaw comes on at Candlemas : I know

Indeed that they will say : " This Galahad
  If he had lived had been a right good knight;
Ah! poor chaste body!" but they will be glad,
  Not most alone, but all, when in their sight

That very evening in their scarlet sleeves
  The gay-dress'd minstrels sing; no maid will talk
Of sitting on my tomb, until the leaves,
  Grown big upon the bushes of the walk,

East of the Palace-pleasaunce, make it hard
  To see the minster therefrom : well-a-day!
Before the trees by autumn were well bared,
  I saw a damozel with gentle play,

Within that very walk say last farewell
　To her dear knight, just riding out to find
(Why should I choke to say it?) the Sangreal,
　And their last kisses sunk into my mind,

Yea, for she stood lean'd forward on his breast,
　Rather, scarce stood; the back of one dear hand,
That it might well be kiss'd, she held and press'd
　Against his lips; long time they stood there, fann'd

By gentle gusts of quiet frosty wind,
　Till Mador· de la porte a-going by,
And my own horsehoofs roused them; they untwined,
　And parted like a dream. In this way I,

With sleepy face bent to the chapel floor,
　Kept musing half asleep, till suddenly
A sharp bell rang from close beside the door,
　And I leapt up when something pass'd me by,

Shrill ringing going with it, still half blind
　I stagger'd after, a great sense of awe
At every step kept gathering on my mind,
　Thereat I have no marvel, for I saw

One sitting on the altar as a throne,
　Whose face no man could say he did not know,
And though the bell still rang, he sat alone,
　With raiment half blood-red, half white as snow.

Right so I fell upon the floor and knelt,
　Not as one kneels in church when mass is said,
But in a heap, quite nerveless, for I felt
　The first time what a thing was perfect dread.

But mightily the gentle voice came down:
　" Rise up, and look and listen, Galahad,
Good knight of God, for you will see no frown
　Upon my face; I come to make you glad.

" For that you say that you are all alone,
　I will be with you always, and fear not
You are uncared for, though no maiden moan
　Above your empty tomb; for Launcelot,

" He in good time shall be my servant too,
    Meantime, take note whose sword first made him
        knight,
And who has loved him alway, yea, and who
    Still trusts him alway, though in all men's sight,

" He is just what you know, O Galahad,
    This love is happy even as you say,
But would you for a little time be glad,
    To make ME sorry long day after day?

" Her warm arms round his neck half throttle Me,
    The hot love-tears burn deep like spots of lead,
Yea, and the years pass quick: right dismally
    Will Launcelot at one time hang his head;

" Yea, old and shrivell'd he shall win my love.
    Poor Palomydes fretting out his soul!
Not always is he able, son, to move
    His love, and do it honour: needs must roll

" The proudest destrier sometimes in the dust,
    And then 'tis weary work; he strives beside
Seem better than he is, so that his trust
    Is always on what chances may betide;

" And so he wears away, my servant, too,
    When all these things are gone, and wretchedly
He sits and longs to moan for Iseult, who
    Is no care now to Palomydes: see,

" O good son Galahad, upon this day,
    Now even, all these things are on your side,
But these you fight not for; look up, I say,
    And see how I can love you, for no pride

" Closes your eyes, no vain lust keeps them down.
    See now you have ME always; following
That holy vision, Galahad, go on,
    Until at last you come to Me to sing

" In Heaven always, and to walk around
    The garden where I am:" he ceased, my face
And wretched body fell upon the ground;
    And when I look'd again, the holy place

Was empty; but right so the bell again
  Came to the chapel-door, there entered
Two angels first, in white, without a stain,
  And scarlet wings, then, after them a bed,

Four ladies bore, and set it down beneath
  The very altar-step, and while for fear
I scarcely dared to move or draw my breath,
  Those holy ladies gently came a-near,

And quite unarm'd me, saying: " Galahad,
  Rest here awhile and sleep, and take no thought
Of any other thing than being glad ;
  Hither the Sangreal will be shortly brought,

" Yet must you sleep the while it stayeth here."
  Right so they went away, and I, being weary,
Slept long and dream'd of Heaven : the bell comes near,
  I doubt it grows to morning.   Miserere !

*Enter Two Angels in white, with scarlet wings ; also Four
  Ladies in gowns of red and green ; also an Angel, bearing in his hands a surcoat of white, with a red cross.*

An Angel.

O servant of the high God, Galahad !
  Rise and be arm'd, the Sangreal is gone forth
Through the great forest, and you must be had
  Unto the sea that lieth on the north :

There shall you find the wondrous ship wherein
  The spindles of King Solomon are laid,
And the sword that no man draweth without sin,
  But if he be most pure : and there is stay'd

Hard by, Sir Launcelot, whom you will meet
  In some short space upon that ship : first, though,
Will come here presently that lady sweet,
  Sister of Percival, whom you well know,

And with her Bors and Percival : stand now,
  These ladies will to arm you.

FIRST LADY, *putting on the hauberke.*
                        Galahad,
That I may stand so close beneath your brow,
    I, Margaret of Antioch, am glad.

                SECOND LADY, *girding him with the sword.*
That I may stand and touch you with my hand,
    O Galahad, I, Cecily, am glad.

                THIRD LADY, *buckling on the spurs.*
That I may kneel while up above you stand,
    And gaze at me, O holy Galahad,
I, Lucy, am most glad.

                FOURTH LADY, *putting on the basnet.*
                    O gentle knight,
That you bow down to us in reverence,
We are most glad, I, Katherine, with delight
    Must needs fall trembling.

                ANGEL, *putting on the crossed surcoat.*
                    Galahad, we go hence,
For here, amid the straying of the snow,
    Come Percival's sister, Bors, and Percival.
                [*The Four Ladies carry out the bed,
                    and all go but* Galahad.

GALAHAD.

How still and quiet everything seems now :
    They come, too, for I hear the horsehoofs fall.

Enter Sir Bors, Sir Percival, *and* his Sister.

Fair friends and gentle lady, God you save !
    A many marvels have been here to-night ;
Tell me what news of Launcelot you have,
    And has God's body ever been in sight.

SIR BORS.

Why, as for seeing that same holy thing,
    As we were riding slowly side by side,
An hour ago, we heard a sweet voice sing,
    And through the bare twigs saw a great light glide,

With many-colour'd raiment, but far off,
  And so pass'd quickly—from the court nought good;
Poor merry Dinadan, that with jape and scoff
  Kept us all merry, in a little wood

Was found all hack'd and dead: Sir Lionel
  And Gauwaine have come back from the great quest,
Just merely shamed; and Lauvaine, who loved well
  Your father Launcelot, at the king's behest

Went out to seek him, but was almost slain,
  Perhaps is dead now; everywhere
The knights come foil'd from the great quest, in vain:
  In vain they struggle for the vision fair.

THE CHAPEL IN LYONESS

Sir Ozana le Cure Hardy.   Sir Galahad.
Sir Bors de Ganys.

Sir Ozana.

All day long and every day,
From Christmas-Eve to Whit-Sunday,
Within that Chapel-aisle I lay,
  And no man came a-near.

Naked to the waist was I,
And deep within my breast did lie,
Though no man any blood could spy,
  The truncheon of a spear.

No meat did ever pass my lips.
Those days—(Alas! the sunlight slips
From off the gilded parclose, dips,
  And night comes on apace.)

My arms lay back behind my head;
Over my raised-up knees was spread
A samite cloth of white and red;
  A rose lay on my face.

Many a time I tried to shout;
But as in dream of battle-rout,
My frozen speech would not well out;
  I could not even weep.

With inward sigh I see the sun
Fade off the pillars one by one,
My heart faints when the day is done,
  Because I cannot sleep.

Sometimes strange thoughts pass through my head;
Not like a tomb is this my bed,
Yet oft I think that I am dead;
  That round my tomb is writ,

" Ozana of the hardy heart,
Knight of the Table Round,
Pray for his soul, lords, of your part;
  A true knight he was found."
Ah! me, I cannot fathom it.   [*He sleeps.*

SIR GALAHAD.

All day long and every day,
Till his madness pass'd away,
I watch'd Ozana as he lay
  Within the gilded screen.

All my singing moved him not;
As I sung my heart grew hot,
With the thought of Launcelot
  Far away, I ween.

So I went a little space
From out the chapel, bathed my face
In the stream that runs apace
  By the churchyard wall.

There I pluck'd a faint wild rose,
Hard by where the linden grows,
Sighing over silver rows
  Of the lilies tall.

I laid the flower across his mouth;
The sparkling drops seem'd good for drouth,
He smiled, turn'd round toward the south,
  Held up a golden tress.

The light smote on it from the west:
He drew the covering from his breast,
Against his heart that hair he prest;
  Death him soon will bless.

SIR BORS.

I enter'd by the western door;
    I saw a knight's helm lying there:
I raised my eyes from off the floor,
    And caught the gleaming of his hair.

I stept full softly up to him;
    I laid my chin upon his head;
I felt him smile; my eyes did swim,
    I was so glad he was not dead.

I heard Ozana murmur low,
    "There comes no sleep nor any love."
But Galahad stoop'd and kiss'd his brow:
    He shiver'd; I saw his pale lips move.

SIR OZANA.

There comes no sleep nor any love;
    Ah me! I shiver with delight.
I am so weak I cannot move;
    God move me to thee, dear, to-night!
Christ help! I have but little wit:
My life went wrong; I see it writ,

" Ozana of the hardy heart,
    Knight of the Table Round,
Pray for his soul, lords, on your part;
    A good knight he was found."
Now I begin to fathom it.   [He dies.

SIR BORS.

Galahad sits dreamily:
What strange things may his eyes see,
Great blue eyes fix'd full on me?
On his soul, Lord, have mercy.

SIR GALAHAD.

Ozana, shall I pray for thee?
  Her cheek is laid to thine;
No long time hence, also I see
  Thy wasted fingers twine

Within the tresses of her hair
  That shineth gloriously,
Thinly outspread in the clear air
  Against the jasper sea.

Printed in the United States
119410LV00001B/25-51/P

9 780851 155449